The Historic Hotels of Scotland

A Select Guide

WENDY ARNOLD

The Historic Hotels of Scotland

A Select Guide

Photographs by
ROBIN MORRISON

THAMES AND HUDSON

*For Eliza McKenzie, my Scottish great-grandmother,
and for Kirsty and Owen*

*Frontispiece: Piper Jimmy Symm, resplendent in full Highland
dress on the steps of the Turnberry Hotel in Ayrshire.*

*Opposite: Superb, home-cooked food and a glass of excellent wine
at Altnaharrie Inn. See p.11.*

Map: Hanni Bailey

Printed and bound in Spain by
Edime/Atanes Lainez-Graphiberia
D.L. M-3.522-1988

Contents

Preface

The grandeur and elegance of a small palace: Inverlochy Castle, Fort William. See p.33.

Scotland's historic hotels are collector's items for the connoisseur traveller: a Victorian extravaganza at the very foot of Britain's highest mountain, a baronial castle in a vast estate with a titled owner, a turn-of-the-century Lutyens mansion beside a world-famous golf-course, a tiny, ancient, white-washed inn nestling on the wooded banks of a tranquil loch. For the gourmet, there are salmon and trout fresh from the rivers, wild game in season – venison, grouse, pheasant – oysters and crayfish and Aberdeen Angus beef. Superb Scottish chefs, trained in France or self-taught, produce with equal skill subtle sauces or scones and shortbread. Open fires blaze in the wide hearths, meals are served on polished tables gleaming with silver and crystal, and spacious, comfortable rooms have views of wildly beautiful scenery and glimpses of red deer and golden eagles.

Having a Scottish great-grandmother had always made me wish to explore the Highlands, but my husband's oil career took us to live abroad for many years in South and Central America, Africa and the Arabian Gulf. Finally we spent four pampered years in the USA, from where we went jetting off to stay in marvellous hotels all over the world. I was often asked by our overseas friends where they should stay in Britain. Exploring hotels for them on visits home, I was appalled to discover how many much-praised places that claimed to offer comfort and culinary expertise had in fact haughty managers, grumpy staff, cold, cramped bedrooms with dusty corners, uninviting bathrooms without showers, inedible food and inflated prices. The shining contrast presented by those hotels who really did have caring staff, clean, comfortable, tastefully furnished rooms and delicious food was so great that I felt that somebody should find out about similar places, and write about them. So I embarked upon several months of intensive country-wide research. I thought it very important not to inform owners until *after* paying my bill about what I was doing, not to accept any hospitality, and where

possible to travel alone, to test a hotel's helpfulness to unaccompanied middle-aged ladies.

The resulting book, *The Historic Country Hotels of England*, proved very popular. Since I had heard rumours of similar splendid hotels in Scotland, I set out to see for myself what they were really like. Asking friends their opinion of Scottish hotels, I found many people who had never visited Scotland supposed the only food to be had would be 'haggis wi' neeps and tatties' (mashed turnips and potatoes), delicious traditional fare which I actually found on offer only once, and then as a novelty. Keen fishermen and golfers liked the thought of the rivers and courses, but had heard tales of cold, bleak accommodation. I was therefore astonished to find how comfortable were many of the hotels, and how outstanding many chefs. I explored several islands, saw many seals and birds, and would exhort anyone with a spirit of adventure and an interest in wildlife to island-hop round the Scottish coast. They will find small hotels and people's homes offering often excellent food and a warm welcome, though not usually great comfort, which is why regretfully I could not include more friendly little island hotels in this book.

Much as I enjoyed exploring the countryside, my happiest memories are of the people I met on my travels, for all the hotels described have welcoming owners or managers who make guests feel instantly at home. They also have historically or architecturally interesting buildings, comfortable bedrooms, modern bathrooms and excellent chefs. All can be reached within a day from Edinburgh and they have been selected to cover as much of the country as possible, allowing visitors to tour Scotland from one to the next. Yet each is quite different from the others. Whether an inexpensive, homely inn or a luxuriously palatial castle, these are the thirty Scottish hotels which I most enjoyed and to which I would most happily return.

General Information

Preparation Booking as far in advance as possible is essential for all the hotels described. Be very specific when booking about any special requirements or diets: if you travel with a great deal of luggage and need a large room, want a wall-mounted shower, a 6-foot bed, accommodation of a standard equivalent to that of friends travelling with you, or if you cannot manage stairs or eat shellfish, say so when booking. Most of these hotels were originally built as private houses, so nothing is standard, which is their charm. Food is fresh each day, so complicated diets need advance notice. Golfers will find courses everywhere: some are public, others require advance arrangements to be made, including the usual letters of introduction and proof of standards of play. Shooting, stalking and fishing are also usually available only with prior notice. It is advisable all year round to take layers of light clothes to build up if necessary; reasonably priced Scottish woollens are readily available.

Terms Since prices can fluctuate, I have given only general guidelines to terms, which should be checked on booking. Ask whether VAT (government tax of 15%) and service are included; hotels sometimes quote these separately. I have calculated prices for two people sharing a room for one night, including 15% VAT and 10% service, dinner (without wine) and Continental breakfast. Several hotels automatically include a full Scottish breakfast (porridge, kippers, scones, etc.) in their charge. (The dollar equivalent is based on a rate of exchange of £1.00 = $1.80.)

Moderate	£90–115 (approx. $162–207)
Medium	£120–140 (approx. $216–252)
Expensive	£145–185 (approx. $261–233)
Very expensive	£190–220 (approx. $342–396)

This does not include *à la carte* prices, drinks, phone calls or other extras. Special bargain weekends, reductions for longer stays and Christmas programmes are sometimes available. Under credit cards, please note that the British Access card is Mastercard in the USA.

Getting there I have noted the nearest convenient airport and rail station to each hotel and have also mentioned whether or not helicopter landing facilities are available. A suggested route by car from Edinburgh is also offered, with approximate distances and journey times. Many of Scotland's cities and much of its most beautiful scenery can be reached on motorways, and require no pioneering spirit. The more adventurous, however, will find a detailed road map of Scotland essential, as the country is divided up by lochs and mountains which can slow down journeys or cause long detours, making less direct routes faster. Driving from London to Edinburgh takes at least a whole day; motor-rail will carry your car there by train; flying takes about an hour, and there is a shuttle service to Edinburgh and Glasgow. Some international airlines fly directly to Prestwick.

Booking ferry crossings is essential. Island hotels will book for you if asked, though if you are planning to visit several islands, reduced 'Car Rover' or 'Island Hopscotch' tickets are advisable. They can be obtained through some travel agents abroad, and through Caledonian MacBrayne Ltd, The Ferry Terminal, Gourock PA19 1QP, Scotland, tel. Gourock (0475) 34531. P & O Ferries, Jamieson's Quay, PO Box 5, Aberdeen, Scotland, tel. Aberdeen (0224) 572615, serve routes to the Orkneys and Shetlands. Hotels in remote areas are often reached by single-track roads, so calculate journey times generously.

Sightseeing I have given some indication of the chief places of interest in a hotel's locality; most hotel owners will happily give more detailed advice. *Historic Houses, Castles and Gardens in Great Britain and Ireland*, published annually in the UK and available from most booksellers and news-stands, gives details of opening times and admission charges. If you plan to visit several National Trust for Scotland properties, remember that membership of the Trust allows free entrance. There are very many wonderful walks; stout shoes and waterproofs are advised even for less serious walkers. I have noted local pubs and small restaurants for light lunches, and more elaborate nearby restaurants to visit during long stays in one place.

Private homes I have included some private homes in this book, as I find them an interesting alternative to hotels. For more information on similar homes, contact In the English Manner, Mawley House, Quenington, Nr. Cirencester, Gloucs. GL7 5BH, England, tel. Cirencester (0285) 75267 or Newport (0239) 77378; telex: 940 12737 ITEM G. Most of the private houses I have described belong to this organization, which inspects those that it recommends, and centralizes booking.

A footnote I am confident that the owners and managers of the hotels and houses I have chosen will be friendly and helpful. If a problem should arise, please point it out to them personally, as they will be glad to be informed; tell them also of anything that specially pleased you about your stay. I too am always grateful for comments and impressions; please write to me care of the publishers.

An alphabetical index of hotels and their locations appears on page 96.

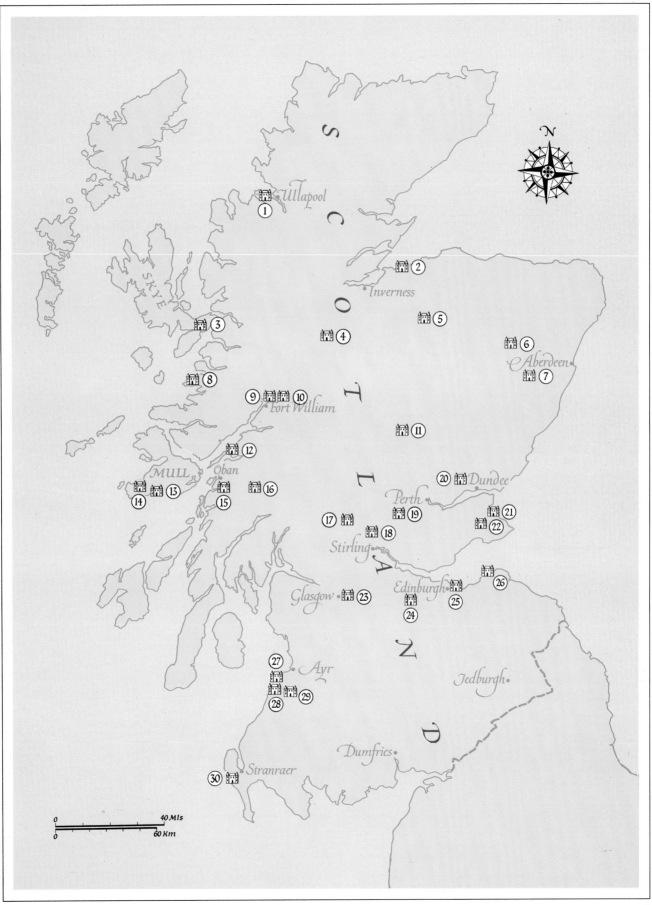

SCOTLAND

SKYE

MULL

N

Ullapool
Inverness
Aberdeen
Fort William
Oban
Perth
Dundee
Stirling
Glasgow
Edinburgh
Jedburgh
Ayr
Dumfries
Stranraer

1
2
3
4
5
6
7
8
9
10
11
12
13
14
15
16
17
18
19
20
21
22
23
24
25
26
27
28
29
30

0   40 Mls
0   60 Km

Creative genius

To say that Altnaharrie Inn is the ultimate escapist's dream would be to insult Fred Brown and Gunn Eriksen, for this remote north-west corner of the Highlands holds everything they most value: solitude, mountains, birds, wildflowers, and the sea lapping almost at their doorstep.

Guests arrive at Ullapool, where they park their cars, telephone, take their luggage down to the small jetty and wait for the inn's modest launch, *Mother Goose*, to appear. This is no place for designer clothes, high heels or matched sets of luggage. The jetties can be seaweedy, and the ten-minute trip is often splashy. Fred, a former vet, quiet and sunburnt, and Gunn, gloriously blonde and Nordic, will greet you, not effusively but with evident pleasure. The tiny whitewashed drovers' inn, which dates back to at least 1745, reveals an artist's eye in every detail. I noticed with delight the grain of the wooden candlestick, the texture of the pottery utensils, the wildflower tucked into the napkin, the white hand-tatted table mats like delicate snowflakes, the massive slabs of timber framing the fireplace in the whitewashed stone wall and the immaculate simplicity of the bedrooms. My room had a heavy antique brass bedhead, a rocking chair with a quilted cushion and a deep louvered cupboard. Beside the bed was a vase of wildflowers and a torch, for the electricity generator is switched off at midnight. The bathroom had plenty of hot water, which ran whisky-coloured by the peat into a gleaming white bath. In the spring there are primroses in the garden and in the evening or early morning you may glimpse a seal in the loch, yards from the inn.

In the evening, having exchanged walking boots and binoculars for something more formal, guests chat together, comfortable in Victorian armchairs in the book-lined sitting room. Gunn, who is a ceramicist by training, cooks what is without question the most delicious food – amateur or professional – that I have ever eaten. Freshly baked bread accompanied cucumber and hawthorn-leaf soup, as sharp as sorrel, but perfectly balanced. Delectable crab and home-made green parsley pasta were followed by breast of wood-pigeon flambéd in armagnac. There were two perfect desserts, rhubarb tart as light as a soufflé, made from slightly crunchy young rhubarb, and a coffee-bean cream confection: I was pressed to try both. It was a dinner cooked with creative genius, eaten with incredulous delight.

You must enjoy the wilderness to come here. There are no ready-made amusements and no television. But for Fred and Gunn, who stay here all year long, and for those who briefly share the fruits of their extraordinarily hard labours, this is life at its most civilized.

A remote hideaway by the sea – guests arrive aboard 'Mother Goose', the Inn's private launch. Gunn Eriksen cooks the exquisite food (above). Overleaf: Wild duck on the nearby seashore, one of the prettily decorated bedrooms and the sitting room where guests gather before dinner.

ALTNAHARRIE INN, Ullapool IV26 2SS, Ross-shire. **Tel.** Dundonnell (085 483) 230. **Telex** No. **Owners** Fred Brown and Gunn Eriksen. **Open** Easter to Oct. **Rooms** 5 double, all with bathroom (1 with hand shower and bath, 2 with bath only, 2 with wall shower only). No phone or TV in rooms. **Facilities** Small lounge, dining room, small garden; loch and mountain views. Fishing, stalking, sailing by arrangement. **Lunch** By arrangement; residents only. **Restrictions** Dogs by arrangement only; not suitable for small children; please no smoking in house or restaurant.

Terms Medium. **Credit cards** No. **Getting there** M9/A9, bypassing Inverness (signposted Ullapool). Take A832 L across Black Isle; after Garve fork R on A835 to Ullapool. 200 miles, approx. 4 hrs. **Helicopter landing** Has been done. **Nearest airport** Inverness. **Nearest rail station** Garve. **Of local interest** Birdwatching, hill walking; Summer Isles; Inverewe Garden and Loch Maree. **Whole day expeditions** Isle of Skye; Loch Ness and Inverness; Island of Honda bird sanctuary. **Refreshments/Dining out** Nothing nearby.

2 The Clifton Hotel

Nairn
Nairnshire

A theatrical treat

The Clifton Hotel is as original and welcoming as its owner, J. Gordon Macintyre, who may be distinguished by his ginger beard and customary kilt, or riding breeches and pink shirt; in the evening he sports a white dinner-jacket and black tie. Mr Macintyre runs the hotel rather as Victorian actor-managers must have run their companies – an apt comparison, since this is the only hotel in Great Britain licensed as a theatre, presented in the round in the dining room in the winter months, when the hotel is closed.

The long creeper-clad stone house looks over a park with pollarded lime trees and a Victorian bandstand to the sea beyond – the higher the room, the better the view, as the owner remarks. I was captivated from the moment my foot crossed the threshold. Just inside the door hang two framed bills for repainting the house in 1877 and 1878, beautifully hand-written in now-faded ink. The stairs rise before one, every inch of wallspace crammed with paintings, prints, collages and posters advertising art exhibitions. The small Green Dining Room, which has beautiful antique silver, is used only at lunchtime, when a light seafood-based menu is served. The drawing room is full of antiques and has gold and maroon wallpaper as used in the Palace of Westminster in 1849. The anteroom to the bar, like the bedrooms, has books everywhere, on shelves and in heaps on tables. There are albums filled with photographs of past theatrical productions, directed by the owner, who also designs the costumes. Dotted about are exquisite ceramic bowls made by his wife, whose studio is next door. Their daughter sometimes helps in the hotel, and their son runs the Edinburgh Puppet Company.

The superb French-inspired food is served in the tiered dining room, which has a grand piano at its centre. The smoked salmon was local, the bread was freshly baked and the turbot was served with herb butter and excellent vegetables. Following a discussion on the exact technique for making the best meringues, I was served two, differently made and both enormous; I also sampled the splendid banana icecream. The coffee arrived in a silver pot, accompanied by a silver dish heaped with tiny macaroons and home-made fudge and chocolates. The selection of wines, said by many to be the best in the north of Scotland, was impressive, and of a standard with the food. A pair of French huntsmen on their annual visit were sitting at a nearby table, eating their meal with evident and discerning enjoyment before retiring early to go stalking at dawn. This hotel is a must for all lovers of art and good food.

The ivy-clad entrance to the Clifton Hotel (opposite, above) and the sumptuous drawing room, lined with ornate Victorian wallpaper and family paintings. Antique silver graces the Green Dining Room (above).

THE CLIFTON HOTEL, Nairn IV12 4HW. **Tel.** Nairn (0667) 53119. **Telex** No. **Owner** J. Gordon Macintyre. **Open** March to Nov. **Rooms** 9 double, 7 single, all with bathroom (bath only). No phone or TV in rooms. **Facilities** Drawing room, writing room, two dining rooms, 1-acre garden, sea and mountain views. Fishing, shooting, sailing, tennis by arrangement. Golf nearby. **Lunch** By arrangement; bar snacks available. **Restrictions** No dogs in public rooms; no smoking in Green Dining Room. **Terms** Moderate. **Credit cards** All major cards. **Getting there** A90 over Forth Bridge, M90/A9 to Inverness, A96 (Aberdeen road) to Nairn. In Nairn turn L at only roundabout. Hotel is on L after $\frac{1}{4}$ mile. 172 miles, approx. $2\frac{1}{2}$ hrs. **Helicopter landing** No. **Nearest airport** Inverness. **Nearest rail station** Nairn. **Of local interest** Inverness and Loch Ness; Culloden Moor; Fort George; Brodie Castle; Cawdor Castle; Elgin (ruined cathedral). **Whole day expeditions** Beauly (woollens and antiques); Fort Augustus; Cairngorms and Highland Wildlife Park; Spey Valley distilleries; Inverewe Garden and Loch Maree. **Refreshments/Dining out** Nothing nearby.

Home of a clan chief

Kinloch Lodge is both the home of clan chief Lord Macdonald of Macdonald and a delightful small hotel tucked into the shelter of its own leafy glen, in a tidy garden framed by twin avenues of towering lime trees that lead down towards the sea. Kinloch Lodge was originally built in the 1680s as a farmhouse. It has two pleasantly proportioned drawing rooms decorated in soft plain autumnal colours (green, gold, russet and deep peach-pink), both with open log fires. The smaller has a large colour television set and both are furnished with comfortable settees, convenient coffee tables, antiques and plenty of books. The views of sea and mountains are especially spectacular at sunset. The dark green walls of the dining room are hung with huge oil paintings of Macdonald ancestors who gaze down on fine crystal, polished tables and sideboards laden with silver entrée dishes. All the bedrooms look out over either sea or wooded hillside, are simply but attractively furnished, have modern bathrooms and are reached by narrow passageways painted pink.

Lady Macdonald, authoress of excellent and highly readable cookery books, which can be purchased and carried off as trophies after a stay here, is often to be seen swathed in a large starched white apron, for she personally cooks the meals, with the help of chef Peter Macpherson. She is fanatical about the freshness of her vegetables and fruit and grows everything she can. Fish and game come from the estate, and she relentlessly tracks down the best and most reliable suppliers of anything it cannot produce. She somehow manages to combine this most successfully with bringing up four children. Lord Macdonald is equally involved with the day-to-day running of Kinloch Lodge, and is on hand to welcome or take leave of guests and to advise on wine or sightseeing.

The dinner was quickly and efficiently served by the friendly local staff. Fresh crab accompanied by tomato and garlic mayonnaise was followed by a roast haunch of the Macdonald's own venison, with vegetables from the garden. Lemon and lime tart, Scottish cheeses and fruit from the orchard concluded a fine meal, and coffee and fudge were served by the fireside. The comprehensive wine list is well explained and sensibly priced. A generous breakfast included freshly squeezed orange juice, one of the best kippers I have ever eaten and scones hot from the oven.

Skye is a wild and beautiful island, famed among climbers for its imposing Cuillin Hills. The little town of Portree is very picturesque and the famous Talisker whisky is produced in a local distillery. A visit to the Clan Donald Centre, at Armadale Castle, ancestral home of the Macdonalds, will tell guests of Kinloch Lodge much about the long family history of their distinguished hosts.

Kinloch Lodge is a clan chief's home on the picturesque Isle of Skye (opposite, above and overleaf). Opposite: Soft autumnal hues in one of the two drawing rooms. Beautiful views from every room survey a prospect of hills, woods, mountains and sea (above).

KINLOCH LODGE, Sleat, Isle of Skye IV43 8QY. **Tel.** Isle Ornsay (047 13) 214/333. **Telex** No. **Owners** Lord and Lady Macdonald. **Open** March to 10 Jan., except 4 days at Christmas. **Rooms** 10 double, all with bathroom, 8 ensuite (baths only). No phone or TV in rooms. **Facilities** 2 drawing rooms, dining room. Gardens, large grounds, sea and mountain views, croquet. Rough shooting, stalking, fishing, sailing by arrangement. **Lunch** No. **Restrictions** Dogs by arrangement only and not in public rooms; not suitable for children under 8; smoking actively discouraged in dining room. **Terms** Medium. Reduced rates for 7 days or longer; substantial winter reductions 1 Nov. to end April (except Easter). **Credit cards** Access/Visa. **Getting there** M9/A9 to Dalwhinnie, L on A889, L on A86 (towards Fort William). At Spean Bridge, R on A82. At Invergarry L on A87 to Kyle of Lochalsh. Take short ferry ride (no booking) to Kyleakin on Isle of Skye. 6 miles on A850, turn L onto A185, hotel drive on L after 6 miles. 204 miles, approx. 5–6 hrs. **Helicopter landing** Yes. **Nearest airport** Broadford (on Skye; will collect if requested) or Inverness. **Nearest rail station** Kyle of Lochalsh. **Of local interest** Loch Scavaig and Loch Coruisk; Cuillin Hills; Portree; Dunvegan Castle; distillery at Carbost; Dunsgaith Castle; Clan Donald Centre at Armadale Castle. **Whole day expeditions** Circuit of Skye; coastal drives on mainland; Strome Castle. **Refreshments** Sligachan Hotel; Three Chimneys Restaurant, Colbost; Skeabost House Hotel. **Dining out** Nothing nearby.

A Highland lodge

Loch Ness, with its intriguing tales of some last survivors from the age of dinosaurs lurking in its mysterious depths, has always held a great fascination for visitors to the Highlands. Scenically spectacular, the steep wooded slopes of its southern shores have remained unspoilt, since only minor roads run along them. There, up among the moorland and heather that lead on into the high mountains, and bordered with groves of silver birch and gnarled mountain pine, are hill lochs, and overlooking one, Loch nan Lann, stands Knockie Lodge.

Built over two hundred years ago as a hunting lodge for the Chief of Clan Fraser, it has been used ever since by sportsmen stalking deer or fishing for brown trout in the loch, or for salmon in nearby rivers or Loch Ness itself. In this remote spot it has been well concealed from the violent and turbulent events in Scotland's long history. Visitors turn from a minor road into a long drive, which winds through woods and past other lochs before turning uphill to the whitewashed walls, towers and grey-slate roofs of Knockie Lodge. Inside, aged pine panelling, open fires, polished antiques and comfortable chintz-covered armchairs, together with a friendly black labrador and the welcoming owners, make one feel that the journey was well worthwhile.

When Ian Milward, formerly a shipping consultant in London, and his wife, Brenda, decided to open a hotel, they searched for many months before they found Knockie Lodge, which they both immediately felt was exactly what they wanted. They set about extensive restoration and refurbishments, making sure that there would be ample hot water for the bathrooms (there are showers wherever the plumbing allows), and creating fresh, simple bed-rooms, with ample clothes-hanging space, good reading lamps, armchairs and books. They installed gleaming new kitchens, found an excellent chef and for waitresses employed charming Scottish girls. Dinner is formally served at polished tables. Delicious smoked trout mousse was followed by lettuce, pea and mint soup and lamb chops with potatoes and leeks in bechamel sauce. After a choice of extravagantly creamy puddings and a good selection of cheeses, coffee and fudge were served by the fireside. No wonder visitors return year after year to this peaceful, attentive hotel.

Opposite: In the hills above Loch Ness, guests can relax in the garden, or among chesterfields and chintz in the sitting room. Local trout (above) are perfectly cooked and artistically presented by the chef.

KNOCKIE LODGE, Whitebridge, Inverness-shire IVI 2UP. **Tel.** Gorthleck (04563) 276. **Telex** No. **Owners** Ian and Brenda Milward. **Open** End April to end Oct. **Rooms** 1 double, 7 twin, 2 single, all with bathroom (4 with wall shower). No phone or TV in rooms. **Facilities** Drawing room, conservatory, dining room, billiard room, loch and mountain views, grounds, own fishing; deer stalking by arrangement. **Lunch** Bar lunches only. **Restrictions** Dogs by arrangement only; not suitable for children under 10. **Terms** Moderate. Reduced rates for 7 nights or longer. **Credit cards** Access/Amex/Eurocard/Mastercard/Visa. **Getting there** M90 to Perth, A9. 10 miles s of Inverness, turn L at Daviot (signposted Fort Augustus) onto B851/862 to Whitebridge. 2 miles after Whitebridge Hotel, turn R at Knockie Lodge sign and follow 2-mile narrow drive. 150 miles, approx. 3 hrs. **Helicopter landing** Yes. **Nearest airport** Inverness. **Nearest rail station** Inverness. **Of local interest** Walking, birdwatching. Inverness and Loch Ness; Culloden Moor; Cawdor Castle; Castle Urquhart. **Whole day expeditions** Fort William; Cairngorms and Highland Wildlife Park. **Refreshments** Grouse and Trout, nr Daviot. **Dining out** Le Chardon, Cromarty.

Lavish comfort

Should you wish to invite friends to join you for a very grand sporting holiday, you could not do better than to take over Tulchan Lodge and its 22,000-acre estate, with pheasant, duck, grouse and partridge shooting, roe deer stalking and 8-mile stretch of the River Spey for fishing. Edward VII, as both Prince of Wales and King, shot and fished here, George V leased it for five years and George VI and his brothers spent holidays here. Theodore Roosevelt, J. P. Morgan and William Vanderbilt were all at one time visitors. You do not, however, need to be a sportsman, nor do you need to hire the whole estate, to enjoy staying at Tulchan Lodge. When I was there, guests were evenly divided between those rising at dawn to go fishing or stalking and those simply enjoying the hotel's splendid facilities.

Tulchan Lodge was built at the turn of the century for lavish comfort. The spacious hall, staircase, landing and library are panelled in oak, hung with oil paintings and furnished with vast studded leather armchairs. The gracious drawing room, which overlooks the river, is filled with antiques; in the dining room guests sit together as at a house party, round a long polished table ornamented with silver game birds. The enormous bedrooms are decorated with antiques, sporting prints and fresh flowers; closets are huge and the luxurious bathrooms have excellent showers.

You will be pampered from the moment you arrive. The butler and his charming staff welcome new arrivals and a groaning tea trolley is set with silver teapots, scones, shortbread and sumptuous cakes. There is an amply stocked bar from which you can help yourself on the honour system, although staff are always on hand to serve drinks if that is preferred. After waking in the morning to a view over manicured lawns and sheltering woods to the River Spey and the heather-clad hills scattered with whitewashed crofts, you come down to a fine array of silver chafing-dishes on the sideboard. There is a comprehensive selection of cereals and fresh juices, and eggs or smoked fish will be prepared for you.

Sportsmen appreciate the gun rooms, fly room, strong room, cold room, drying room and sporting rifle zeroing range. They may lease from the same owners the 80,000-acre estate of Mar Lodge on Deeside, built by Queen Victoria for one of her granddaughters, or Amhuinnsuidhe Castle and 60,000 acres on the Island of Harris. These are not open to hotel guests, who in any case would probably prefer the comforts of Tulchan Lodge, a setting which has proved itself fit for kings.

Opposite and above: Leather-studded armchairs, fine paintings and delicious malt whisky give Tulchan Lodge a country-club style with a distinctive Scots flavour.

TULCHAN LODGE, Grantown-on-Spey, Advie, Morayshire PH26 3PW. **Tel.** Advie (08075) 200. **Telex** 75405 (TULCHAN G). **Owner** Tulchan Estates. **Estate secretary** Fiona Sinclair. **Open** Mid-April to early Oct. Winter season for shooting parties only. **Rooms** 11 double, all with bathroom (with showers: 6 as separate units, 5 wall-mounted) and direct-dial phone. TV on request. Separate cottage has 1 double bedroom, living room and kitchenette. **Facilities** Library, drawing room, dining room, billiard room, gun room, fly room, strong room, drying room, cold store, rifle range, tennis court. 22,000-acre sporting estate with 8 miles of fishing on River Spey (both banks), roe deer stalking, pheasant, duck, grouse and partridge shooting. Gardens, woods, moors. **Lunch** By arrangement only. **Restrictions** Dogs in outside kennels only. **Terms** Expensive. **Credit cards** No. **Getting there** A90 over Forth Bridge, M90/A9/A95 to Grantown. B9102, hotel on L after 7 miles. 145 miles, approx. 2½ hrs. **Helicopter landing** Yes. **Nearest airport** Inverness. **Nearest rail station** Aviemore. **Of local interest** Inverness and Loch Ness; whisky distilleries in Spey Valley; Cairngorms and Highland Wildlife Park; skiing at Aviemore. **Whole day expeditions** Golf at Dornech; Braemar Castle. **Refreshments** Nothing nearby. **Dining out** The Clifton Hotel, Nairn (see p. 15).

A welcoming family castle

One of the many pleasures offered by Scotland is the opportunity to visit a castle filled with mementoes of a family and a clan gathered over several centuries, including portraits in which you can trace the features of your host. Castle Forbes is the seat of Clan Forbes, whose head, Lord Forbes, is the Premier Baron of Scotland. The family crest incorporates three bears' heads, and a roughly carved granite head of a bear is set into the wall of the Yellow Dining Room, near the sword wielded by Black Angus Forbes at the Battle of Tillieangus in 1571. More recent memorabilia include delicate watercolours of game birds by the present Lord Forbes, and souvenirs of the worldwide travels of his son and daughter-in-law Jonathan and Nicky, who, with their three small children and two friendly dogs, are the castle's present inhabitants. They have recently completed the enormous undertaking of redecorating and refurbishing much of the building. Nicky, also of distinguished lineage, is very enthusiastic about her garden, which supplies not only flowers for the beautiful arrangements that decorate the rooms, but also fresh vegetables to accompany fish and game from the estate at their pleasantly formal dinner parties.

The present castle was rebuilt between 1815 and 1820 around a 17th-century core, and stands amid 5000 wooded, park-like acres overlooking the River Don. Lofty ceilings and tall windows, crystal chandeliers and huge fireplaces lend distinction to the gracious main rooms, which are ideal for large or very formal parties. House guests may also use a small family sitting room, furnished with comfortable chairs and a colour television. My bedroom had a marvellously comfortable Victorian bed, with fine embroidered linen and soft down pillows, an electric blanket and electric fire for chilly evenings, a courtesy tea-tray with fresh shortbread, flowers from the garden and good antique furniture. The bathroom opposite was well provided with toiletries, and had the largest white towels I have ever seen; there was also a dressing-room with its own single bed. This is an excellent place for people who travel with mountains of luggage. The bed was turned down, and nightclothes laid out at night, the tall shutters closed, and curtains drawn. Opening them in the morning revealed a cock pheasant strolling through the dewy grass.

Since this is a private house, it is important to book well in advance: you cannot just arrive at the front door expecting a room for the night. I found Castle Forbes warmly welcoming and took away highly enjoyable memories of my stay with the Forbes family.

Ancestral portraits, family silver and crystal chandeliers adorn the dining and drawing rooms within the sturdy turrets and battlements of Castle Forbes (opposite and above).

CASTLE FORBES, Alford, Aberdeenshire AB3 8BL. **Tel.** Alford (0336) 2509. **Telex** No. **Owners** The Hon. Jonathan and Mrs Nichola Forbes. **Open** All year, except Feb. NB Private house, advance bookings only. **Rooms** 1 double, with bathroom, 2 twins with single-bed dressing room and separate bathroom each. No showers. No TV or phone in rooms. **Facilities** Large drawing room, sitting room with colour TV, radio and cassette player, dining room. Private parkland, woods, river, views. Own fishing; shooting and stalking by arrangement. **Lunch** By arrangement only. **Restrictions** Dogs in kennels only. **Terms** Medium. **Credit cards** No. **Getting there** A90 over Forth Bridge, M90. Just before Perth, turn R for M85/A85/A972/A92 to Aberdeen. In Aberdeen, L on A944 (Alford road). After approx. 23 miles, turn R at Whitehouse onto B992 (Insch road). After approx. 2 miles, turn R 50 yds after crossing river, on to tarmac drive. 130 miles, approx $2\frac{3}{4}$ hrs. **Helicopter landing** Yes. **Nearest airport** Aberdeen. **Nearest rail station** Insch. **Of local interest** Castle Frazer; Craigievar Castle; Kildrummy Castle and garden; Fyvie Castle. **Whole day expeditions** Circuit of the above castles; grounds of Balmoral Castle and Royal Deeside; distilleries in Spey Valley; Aberdeen. **Refreshments** Forbes Arms Hotel, Bridge of Alford; Grant Arms, Monymusk. **Dining out** Meldrum House, Old Meldrum.

On royal Deeside

Visitors to the Scottish Highlands are sometimes startled to come across members of the royal family shopping in local villages when taking a holiday at their castle in Balmoral to enjoy fishing the local rivers, here on what is known as Royal Deeside. One of the tributaries of the Dee, the Water of Feugh, famous for its bridge from which salmon can be seen leaping up the falls, runs through the grounds of Invery House. The long drive follows the river's tree-lined course, and widens to a broad sweep of gravel in front of the entrance. The stone-flagged hall is filled with stuffed badgers, eagles, herons and otters, enormous prize salmon in glass cases, antlered heads, fishing rods, reels, and racks of shotguns. The long, gracious inner hall, with elegant antiques and hangings, leads to the enormous drawing room, furnished with pretty flowered fabrics. There is also a small bar bristling with bottles and a conference room. The two dining rooms have graceful arched windows and – unusually – very comfortable wing chairs.

Stewart and Sheila Spence, owners of three hotels in Aberdeen, had for long wanted to own the sort of country house hotel they had always enjoyed visiting in Britain and France. Invery House, then in private hands and sadly run-down, gave them the challenge they sought. They hunted out antiques in sales, selected different tiles for each bathroom and different fabrics for each bedroom and installed excellent free-standing showers. Since Sir Walter Scott had once been a guest in the house, they decided to name the bedrooms after his novels. The rooms vary in size and shape but all have plenty of space for easy chairs. One has a sitting room in a round turret and a four-poster bed, another has antique carved furniture. Everything an international traveller might hope to find is there: a bedside phone, with another in the bathroom, television, plenty of magazines and books, a decanter of sherry, fruit (with knife, plate and napkin), fresh shortbread, excellent toiletries, towelling robes, linen sheets, a big clothes closet and a perfuming bowl of pot pourri. Refreshments appear rapidly when requested, served in delicate china or crystal. The bedrooms look out over smooth lawns, a walled garden and a wooded hillside; at night, the only sound is the soothing swish of the river over pebbles. The chef was formerly at Inverlochy Castle (see page 33) and dinner was, as might therefore be expected, creative, delicious and served in generous portions. Invery House is a welcome luxurious newcomer to the Scottish hotel scene.

Above: Highland sporting trophies in the hall. Opposite: A bedroom with bright brass bedstead, flounced and buttoned easy chair and graceful sash windows looks out onto the tranquil setting.

INVERY HOUSE, Bridge of Feugh, Banchory, Kincardineshire AB3 3NJ. **Tel.** Banchory (03302) 4782. **Telex** 73737. **Owners** Stewart and Sheila Spence. **Manager** Tom Ward. **Open** All year. **Rooms** 1 suite, 12 double, 1 single, all with bathroom (all but 1 with wall shower), direct-dial phone, radio, TV. **Facilities** 2 drawing rooms, bar, billiard room, conference room, restaurant, walled garden, putting green, extensive wooded grounds with river, private salmon and sea trout fishing. Stalking and grouse and pheasant shooting on local private estates by arrangement. **Lunch** Yes. **Restrictions** Dogs in kennels only; no children under 8. **Terms** Expensive. Reduced rates Oct. to March. Special Christmas and New Year programmes. **Credit cards** Access/Amex/Diners/Visa. **Getting there** A90 over Forth Bridge, M90/M85/A85/A972/A92 to Stonehaven. L on A957 to Crathes, L on A93 to Banchory, L on B974 to Invery House. 100 miles, approx. 2½ hrs. **Helicopter landing** Yes. **Nearest airport** Aberdeen. **Nearest rail station** Aberdeen. **Of local interest** Crathes Castle; Drum Castle; grounds of Balmoral Castle and Royal Deeside; Grampian mountains. **Whole day expeditions** Spey Valley whisky distilleries; Aberdeen; Braemar. **Refreshments** Potarch Inn, Potarch. **Dining out** Castle Forbes (see p. 25), by arrangement only.

Splendour restored

There were huge bowls of daffodils in the hall when I visited Arisaig House in the spring. Outside, this imposing grey stone mansion, designed in 1864 by William Morris's friend Philip Webb, looks like a medieval manor house, but the interior was totally refurbished in the 1930s with the elegance, excellent craftsmanship and solid oak joinery of that period. This is a gracious house, always filled with fresh flowers, with large, light, well-proportioned rooms, deep, comfortable armchairs in well-separated groups and a spacious dining room panelled in cherry wood, overlooking a leafy hillside. Each bedroom is different, some furnished with antiques, others with modern wicker and bamboo, all inviting and comfortable. The bathrooms are good and are equipped with hand showers.

John and Ruth Smither bought Arisaig House in 1981 and opened it as a hotel a year later to the day. Their son-in-law is the excellent chef and his varied menus change daily. Local produce, together with fruit, vegetables and herbs from their own walled garden, ensures the freshness of everything served, and there is a well-chosen wine list offering excellent value. The gardens are the family's special pride, since they have won them back from long neglect to their original Victorian splendour. Huge banks of rhododendrons frame the rose terrace and delightful walks can be taken on smooth bright green carpets of moss beneath the overhanging trees.

The dedicated walker can climb up to a spring-fed loch above the hotel to enjoy the best view of mountains and sea, dotted with little islands, or stroll down to find the same view from the shore. To do this, you have to cross several fields. Entering the first, I was extremely disconcerted when a large flock of sheep and their new-born lambs charged toward me, bleating loudly. The sheep in the next field, alerted by the din, bunched by the gate to await my arrival. Totally disconcerted, I retreated, and never reached the shore. The Smithers, amused, told me that at lambing time the shepherd feeds the sheep, who probably thought I was bringing them extra rations. At other times of the year one is, I was assured, left in peace.

Guests may, if they wish, arrive by train, rather grandly requesting that it stop specially at Beasdale. Steam trains also run on this scenically spectacular line as a holiday attraction. From the hotel you may follow the famous road to the Isles, crossing by ferry to the Isle of Skye. It was at Arisaig that Bonnie Prince Charlie landed to stage his uprising, and from here he fled to France, never to return.

Granite walls and rose gardens at Arisaig House (opposite). Lavishly carved balustrades line the staircase (above). Overleaf: Sheep grazing the fields between the house and the sea, and one of the sunny bedrooms. Coffee is served in the grounds amid brilliant flowers and mellow stone walls.

ARISAIG HOUSE, Beasdale, Arisaig, Inverness-shire PH39 4NR. **Tel.** Arisaig (06875) 622. **Telex** 777279 ARISAI G. **Owners** John and Ruth Smither. **Open** Easter to end Oct. **Rooms** 13 double, 1 single, all with bathrooms (incl. hand showers), direct-dial phone and TV. **Facilities** Large inner hall, drawing room, morning room, dining room, bar, 20 acres of wooded grounds and gardens, mountain views, croquet, fishing by arrangement. **Lunch** Yes. **Restrictions** No dogs; children over 10 welcome; no smoking in dining room. **Terms** Medium. **Credit cards** Access/Amex/Visa. **Getting there** M9 to Stirling, exit 10, A84/85 to Crianlarich, A82 through Fort William towards Inverness. Turn L on to A830 (signposted Mallaig). After approx. 30 miles, hotel on L, 1 mile past Beasdale station. 165 miles, approx. 4 hrs. **Helicopter landing** Yes. **Nearest airport** Inverness. **Nearest rail station** Beasdale (request stop). **Of local interest** Prince Charles's cave and beach, from 1745 uprising; white sand beaches; Ben Nevis, highest mountain in Great Britain. **Whole day expeditions** Isle of Skye from Mallaig ferry; islands of Muck, Eigg, Rhum and Canna from Arisaig; Ardnamurchan peninsula; Inverness and Loch Ness; steam trains of West Highland railway. **Refreshments** Old Library, Arisaig. **Dining out** Inverlochy Castle (see p. 33).

Legendary perfection

Inverlochy Castle has been so universally praised that I set out to visit it with great reservations. Could anywhere be so perfect? It can be, and it is.

The castle is an imposing grey stone mansion built in the 1860s and embellished with turrets, towers and battlements. Inside it displays the grandeur and elegance of a small palace. The Great Hall has immensely high painted ceilings, the drawing room is enormous, with elaborate plasterwork and floor-to-ceiling windows, the dining room glitters with silver and the billiard room is hung with an impressive collection of horned trophies of the chase. The setting is idyllic, for the castle sits amid a vast sea of rhododendrons (glorious in spring) and overlooks its own loch in a 500-acre estate ringed by Britain's highest and most majestic mountains. Queen Victoria stayed here for a week and wrote in her diary, 'I never saw a lovelier or more romantic spot'.

Yet the magic of Inverlochy Castle does not lie only in its scenery and architecture. As you drive up to the entrance porch, manager Michael Leonard and a white-jacketed butler hasten out to greet even the first-time guest by name. As though you were the eagerly awaited owner, they enquire with real concern about the journey up, whisk away the luggage and instantly produce a well-laden tea tray. After conducting you to your room to be absolutely certain everything there is as it should be, and urging you to lift the telephone if you require anything at all, they leave you to contemplate the evening's menu. My spacious bedroom was simply but charmingly furnished with attractive pale yellow chintz curtains, a six-foot bed and a large range of fitted cupboards. The modern bathroom was generously equipped.

A wide straight staircase with massive wooden banisters leads down into the Great Hall. Drinks are

served here or in the drawing room before dinner, accompanied by delicious freshly baked appetisers. The expertly cooked meal was served in the dining room, overlooking loch and mountains, where we were waited upon by charming local girls. There is a suggested menu, with three or four alternatives to each main course, and a superb and most comprehensive list of excellent wines judiciously priced. The Head Chef, Graham Newbould, was the Prince of Wales's chef for five years before joining Inverlochy Castle. Guests chatted together over coffee and owner Grete Hobbs joined us briefly. Her late husband bought the castle in 1944 and for many years it was their family home. With its fresh flowers, fine china, lovely antiques, friendly, helpful staff and superb cooking and housekeeping, this is the atmosphere it still retains today.

Inverlochy is an imposing mansion from which to survey the misty grandeur of the Highlands (opposite, above). Magnificent antlers decorate the billiard room (opposite, below). Overleaf: Drinks are served in the Great Hall and drawing room before dinner.

INVERLOCHY CASTLE, Torlundy, Fort William, Inverness-shire PH33 6SN. **Tel.** Fort William (0397) 2177/8. **Telex** 776229. **Owner** Mrs Grete Hobbs. **Manager** Michael Leonard. **Open** Mid-March to mid-Nov. **Rooms** 2 suites, 14 double or twin, all with bathroom (incl. wall shower), radio, TV and direct-dial phone. **Facilities** Drawing room, sitting room, Great Hall, dining room, 500-acre grounds with own loch and view of Ben Nevis. Billiards, hard tennis court. Golf at Fort William; stalking and fishing by arrangement. **Lunch** Yes. **Restrictions** No dogs; guests asked to refrain from smoking in dining room. **Terms** Very expensive. **Credit cards** Access/Visa.

Getting there M9 to Stirling. Exit 10 for A84 to Lochearnhead via Callander. L on to A85 to Crianlarich. R on to A82 to Fort William, continue for 12 miles, ignoring signs to Inverlochy. Castle entrance on L. 135 miles, approx. 3½ hrs. **Helicopter landing** Yes. **Nearest airport** Inverness. **Nearest rail station** Fort William. **Of local interest** Fort William; Glencoe; Mallaig; Glenfinnan and Loch Shiel. **Whole day expeditions** Isles of Skye and Mull; Glen Shiel; Glen Carron; Inverness and Loch Ness. **Refreshments** Nothing nearby. **Dining out** Factor's House, on Inverlochy estate (see p. 37); Airds Hotel, Appin (see p. 43).

Below Ben Nevis

In the course of many visits to Scotland I had passed by Ben Nevis several times without ever having a good view of Britain's highest mountain, for it was always shrouded in deep mist. But when I came down to breakfast at The Factor's House and looked out of the dining room window, there it was, splendid in the June sunshine, still with a small cap of snow. Peter Hobbs, son of Inverlochy Castle's owner, Grete Hobbs, has had the excellent idea of totally refurbishing the factor's cottage on the edge of his mother's large estate and making from it a small, simple and friendly hotel. (A factor is an estate manager.)

This is a most beautiful part of the west coast, just outside Fort William, at the foot of the Great Glen. The hotel has a modest garden, with a lawn, terrace and tubs of flowers. Inside are two sitting rooms with open fires, a pine-clad dining room built out to capture the view and double-glazed against draughts, like the rest of the hotel. The small bedrooms, furnished with fresh, sprigged cottons, have duvets on the beds, colour televisions, direct-dial phones, ample cupboard space and full-length mirrors. The good modern bathrooms are all equipped with showers.

The hotel has an enjoyably informal atmosphere, although Peter and his young manager punctiliously don kilts and silver-buttoned jackets each night to serve dinner, and guests, made equally welcome at Inverlochy Castle any evening, usually also change from casual day-wear to jacket and tie or dress. A short menu is chalked up daily on blackboards in the dining room and the good home cooking is pleasantly served. Dishes of vegetables are put on the tables, the portions are ample and traditional British puddings are a speciality. Next morning's porridge with cream was especially good.

Throughout the hotel are prints of famous Victorian explorers and adventurous moments in their lives. Peter Hobbs is a Fellow of the Royal Geographical Society, and is himself a keen explorer and yachtsman – he hopes one day to circumnavigate the globe. A large amiable black labrador greets guests, though he knows he may not put paw into the dining room. Visitors can set forth for a day's journey to the lovely Western Isles of Skye or Mull, certain that they will be warmly welcomed on their return, and that somebody interested in hearing of their discoveries will be waiting to exchange travellers' tales.

Welcoming, comfortable interiors at The Factor's House (opposite), a cosy retreat amid rugged scenery. Above is one of the local Highland cattle.

THE FACTOR'S HOUSE, Torlundy, Fort William, Inverness-shire PH33 6SN. **Tel.** Fort William (0397) 5767. **Telex** 776229 (AHN F H). **Owner** Peter Hobbs FRGS. **Open** All year, except mid-Dec. to mid-March. **Rooms** 6 double, all with bathroom (5 with bath and wall shower, 1 with shower only), TV and direct-dial phone. **Facilities** 2 small sitting rooms, dining room, small garden, tennis court, sailing by prior arrangement. **Lunch** Yes (residents only). **Restrictions** No dogs; no children under 6 in dining room at dinner. **Terms** Moderate. ½ litre of wine included. **Credit cards** Access/Amex/Diners/Visa. **Getting there** As Inverlochy Castle (p. 33); hotel is on L of A82 just beyond the sign for Inverlochy Castle. 135 miles, approx. 3½ hrs. **Helicopter landing** No. **Nearest airport** Inverness. **Nearest rail station** Fort William. **Of local interest/Whole day expeditions** See Inverlochy Castle (p. 33). **Refreshments** Many small restaurants in Fort William; the hotel will provide further information. **Dining out** Inverlochy Castle (p. 33).

11 Strathgarry House

Killiecrankie
Perthshire

Warm hospitality

Sebastian and Henrietta Thewes are enormously hospitable people. Staying with them in their private home, Strathgarry House, you will be swept irresistibly into a whirl of friends, children, dogs, exciting outings and marvellous food, feeling that you have known the family forever.

The house stands on a bluff, with beautiful views on all sides, up to the mountains and down to their ½ mile of salmon fishing on the River Garry. Mid-Victorian, with much older cellars, it is near to the famous 1689 battlefield where 'Bonnie Dundee' triumphed for the Jacobites. This large, rambling, comfortably-lived-in family house has a wide hall, a huge kitchen, where visitors are always welcome, high-ceilinged dining rooms and a big double drawing room with an open fireplace. Antiques, fine porcelain, prints, paintings, masses of fresh flowers and ancient Persian tribal rugs are scattered about. Bas, who works for Christie's Fine Art Auctioneers, is an enthusiastic fisherman and shot; Henrietta, kind and welcoming, is an amazing organizer. The day I arrived she had had a picnic lunch with her mother, attended a Committee Meeting in Perth, cooked and iced a birthday cake in the shape of a Wrigley's Chewing Gum packet for her son's tenth birthday, consoled their cherished Australian au-pair girl, who was leaving next day, and cooked a superb dinner party for ten, reasoning that since she was cooking anyway, she might as well invite 'some local gentry' for me to meet. That one guest had to rush off to a favourite cow's calving just as we sat down to dinner in no way ruffled her calm. This was one of the best meals I have ever eaten in Scotland. A perfect sole soufflé, flavoured with hazelnut and orange zest and served with hollandaise, was followed by meltingly tender roe deer venison cooked with juniper,

cinnamon and bacon, accompanied by a sauce of pan juices, cream and red-currant jelly. Home-made kirsch icecream in a fluted tuile with bittersweet Italian morello cherries preserved in amaretto was equally memorable and the meal concluded with an excellent selection of cheeses. Breakfast, brought up on a tray, was just as good.

My large bedroom had a massive Victorian bed with a good mattress, a brilliant Victorian velvet patchwork coverlet and fine linen sheets. The vast bathroom was adorned with stuffed shaggy heads of gnu and eland on scarlet Stuart dress tartan wallpaper; the curtains were dark green Stuart hunting tartan. Visitors wishing to stay, or lunch as they pass by, must book well in advance, either directly or through In the English Manner (see page 7), which can suggest other private houses and hosts in Scotland, though surely no one is more delightful than the unforgettable Thewes.

This delightful family house is poised between mountains and the banks of the River Garry (opposite). There is excellent cooking, with local game and fish (above). Overleaf: Linen sheets, Stuart tartan decor and a beautiful walled garden.

STRATHGARRY HOUSE, Killiecrankie, Pitlochry, Perthshire PH16 5LJ. **Tel.** Blair Atholl (079681) 466/216. **Telex** No. **Owners** Sebastian and Henrietta Thewes. **Open** All year. **Rooms** 5 double, 1 with ensuite bathroom, 1 with ensuite wall shower, 1 with private bathroom, 2 with shared bathroom. No phone or TV in bedrooms. **Facilities** Drawing room, dining room, 10-acre grounds, 1¼-acre walled garden, woods (incl. ancient battleground), tennis, ½-mile of salmon fishing on the River Garry. Stalking, shooting, fishing on the River Tay and sailing can all be arranged. **Lunch** By arrangement. **Restrictions** None. **Terms** Medium. **Credit cards** No. **Getting there** A90 over Forth Bridge, M90/A9. Just after Pitlochry turn L at signpost for Killiecrankie. In Killiecrankie turn L opposite post office. Cross railway and river, bear R along river for 1 mile, turn L into drive. 85 miles, approx. 1½ hrs. **Helicopter landing** Yes. **Nearest airport** Edinburgh. **Nearest rail station** Pitlochry (courtesy car will collect by arrangement). **Of local interest** Pitlochry (drama festival and Highland Games in summer); Blair Castle; Glamis Castle; Scone Palace. **Whole day expeditions** Edinburgh; Inverness; Loch Tay; Loch Tummel; golf at Gleneagles, St Andrews, Carnoustie, Rosemont, Pitlochry and Blair Atholl (9 holes). Grampian mountains. **Refreshments/Dining out** Nothing nearby.

Gourmet delights

A map drawn in 1747 marks a 'Ferry Inn' at the place where drovers arrived with their cattle from the Island of Lismore, on their way to market on the mainland. This same inn is now the friendly Airds Hotel. It stands in the wildly beautiful area of the Western Highlands known as Lorn, which has mountains, lochs, sandy bays, many little islands off the coast and a history going back to the Stone Age. The owner of Airds Hotel, Eric Allen, is a delightful, sturdy Scotsman, who always wears the kilt, as do his staff. Betty Allen, his wife, gracious and tranquil, is rarely seen, as she is the chef, both creating and cooking the outstanding dishes which have won her many awards, including that of Chef Laureate of the Academy of British Gastronomes.

As you enter the little, low whitewashed inn, a display of Victorian stuffed squirrels and badgers greets you at the top of the stairs. The original inn parlour to your right is large and traditionally furnished with comfortable velvet and brocaded chairs. A cheerful fire is lit in the hearth on chilly days and there are plenty of books to read. A narrow flower-filled conservatory with wicker armchairs at the front of the hotel borders the quiet road that leads to the village nearby. Contented guests can sit here to take the sun and revel in the view of mountains, sea, lighthouse and sailing boats. The trim garden ends promisingly in an extensive, well-stocked vegetable plot and hen-run. Large panes of plate glass have replaced the original tiny windows of the dining room, so that the view and the sunsets can be enjoyed during meals. Dinner was memorable: excellent delicate green mange-tout soup, freshly baked bread and succulent local prawns were followed by tender

Scottish beef rolled in fresh herbs, accompanied by cabbage delicately flavoured with juniper, courgettes with garlic and potatoes cooked in cream. A mango mousse with a faint hint of ginger appeared in a mango coulis, and the delicious coffee was served with 'tablet', traditional Scottish fudge.

I spent a most comfortable night under the sloping ceiling of my attic bedroom, which had a good firm bed and a large mirrored hanging cupboard. The peach-coloured towels in the impeccable bathroom matched the small peach roses in the wallpaper. The only sound was the cry of gulls. The staff were attentive, helpful and efficient, the food – including the breakfast – exceptionally good. It is not surprising to learn that the same guests return year after year.

Flowers and drystone walls without, cosy armchairs within (opposite). Chef Laureate Betty Allen creates award-winning dishes (above) – gourmet sophistication in a truly breathtaking setting (overleaf).

THE AIRDS HOTEL, Port Appin, Appin, Argyll PA38 4DF. **Tel.** Appin (063 173) 236. **Telex** No. **Owners** Eric and Betty Allen. **Open** March to Jan. **Rooms** 13 double, all with bathroom (12 with bath, 1 with shower). No TV or phone in rooms. **Facilities** 2 lounges, 2 dining rooms, conservatory, small bar (residents only), ½-acre garden by loch (with seats), loch and mountain views. Golf at Oban (25 miles). Sea and loch sailing by arrangement. **Lunch** Yes. **Restrictions** Dogs by arrangement only; no children under 5; no smoking in dining room. **Terms** Medium. **Credit cards** No. **Getting there** M9 to Stirling. Exit 10 for A84 to Lochearnhead. A85 to Crianlarich, A82 to South Ballachulish. s on A828 along coast. After approx. 12 miles, turn R to Port Appin. 125 miles, approx. 3½ hrs. **Helicopter landing** Yes (24 hrs. notice). **Nearest airport** Glasgow. **Nearest rail station** Oban. **Of local interest** This area is the setting for Robert Louis Stevenson's *Catriona* and *Kidnapped*; Oban (glass factory); Glencoe; Fort William (shopping for woollens) and Ben Nevis. Port at Appin; ferry to island of Lismore; Barcaldine Castle; Dunstaffnage Castle. **Whole day expeditions** Islands of Mull and Iona; Staffa and Fingal's Cave; Inverary Castle; Loch Sunart and Ardnamurchan peninsula. **Refreshments** Taychreggan Hotel, Kilchrenan (see p. 53); Longhouse Buttery, Isle of Luing. **Dining out** Inverlochy Castle, Fort William (see p. 33); Glenfeochan House, Kilmore (see p. 51).

An island retreat

Having often enjoyed holidays on the Isle of Mull, Robin and Sue Blockey decided that they would like to buy a small weekend cottage there. Arriving to look it over one sunny day in early spring, they fell hopelessly in love with this corner of the island, and bought not only the cottage but a substantial house with ten wooded acres and an incomparable view. Robin was then a career officer in the Royal Air Force, so deciding what to do next was a problem. Their lives had always involved frequent moves and redecoration, formal entertainment and dinner parties. They therefore decided to refurbish totally their newly acquired Georgian farmhouse with its Victorian hunting lodge additions. They added a large conservatory to the dining room to take advantage of the view, gathered together their families' best antiques, organized Robin's departure from the RAF, and opened Tiroran House as a hotel.

It has been enormously hard work, but they have never regretted their decision. Robin's administrative training means that everything runs with smooth efficiency. Sue produces a different menu each night, based on the day's freshest local produce. Curried apple soup with croutons, pork fillet with savoury apricots, casseroled potatoes, buttered cabbage with celery and sweet corn with paprika were followed by a choice of plum alaska, mocha bavarois, or hot peach, raspberry and brandy tart – I cannot deny having sampled them all. Everything was well-seasoned and delicious and the wine list was well-chosen, balanced and reasonably priced. A vine planted in the sunny conservatory has so flourished that in summer dinner is served under a canopy of green leaves and plump purple bunches of grapes.

The close-carpeted house is kept spotlessly clean and fires burn cheerfully in the grates of the small front and back sitting rooms, which overlook a scrupulously kept garden. Flower-filled borders lie beside a small stream and waterfalls, all stoutly fenced and walled against encroaching deer, to which end you are exhorted always to close the entrance gate behind you.

My warm and comfortable bedroom was furnished with a gold fitted carpet and matching chintz curtains and bedcover in soft yellow and dark blue. The wardrobe and dresser were delightful antiques and as well as fresh flowers from the garden and plenty of books, a desk filled with helpful tourist information, a courtesy tea tray and masses of toiletries were thoughtfully provided. This is a welcoming, peaceful setting in which to relax, enjoy long walks, tour Mull and Iona and enjoy the house-party atmosphere with your fellow guests.

The leafy, vine-covered conservatory is the ideal setting for a summer meal (opposite); outside lie beautiful gardens and views over the Isle of Mull (above).

TIRORAN HOUSE, Isle of Mull, Argyll PA39 6ES. **Tel.** Tiroran (06815) 232. **Telex** No. **Owners** Wing Commander Robin Blockey and Sue Blockey. **Open** Early May to early Oct. **Rooms** 7 double and annexe with 1 double and 1 single, all with bathroom (bath and hand shower) and radio. No phone or TV in bedrooms. **Facilities** Drawing room, sitting room, dining room, conservatory, sea and mountain views, 40-acre grounds, woods and garden, croquet. Stalking and fishing by arrangement. **Lunch** By arrangement only. **Restrictions** Dogs by arrangement only, leashed in grounds, not in public rooms; not usually children under 10. **Terms** Moderate. Reduced rates for 3 days or longer; refund of ferry fare for visits of 5 days or longer. **Credit cards** No. **Getting there** M9 to Stirling. Exit 10 for A84 to Lochearnhead, A85 to Crianlarich, A82 to Tyndrum, A85 to Oban. Ferry to Mull ($\frac{3}{4}$-hr. crossing; cars must book). From ferry, turn L on A849 towards Fionnphort. After 15 miles, turn R on B8035. After 5 miles, L to Tiroran, entrance to hotel after 1 mile. NB single-track roads on Mull, allow ample time. Edinburgh to Oban, 130 miles, approx. 3 hrs. **Helicopter landing** Yes. **Nearest airport** Glasgow. **Nearest rail station** Oban. **Of local interest** Isles of Iona, Treshnish and Staffa. 200 miles of coastal scenic single-track roads on Mull; wildlife expeditions; Tobermory. **Whole day expeditions** As above, also via non-bookable 10 min. ferry Fishnish–Lochaline for Morvern and Ardnamurchan peninsulas. **Refreshments/Dining out** Many small places: enquire from owner.

14 Ardfenaig House

Bunessan
Isle of Mull

Civilized calm

Famous for its glorious scenery, the Isle of Mull seems to have a special attraction for interesting and unexpected people. An Old Etonian makes and sells jams and chutney, under the name of Gremlin, an ex-stockbroker and his wife run a small Jersey dairy herd and deliver the milk themselves, and Ardfenaig House is owned by a former Oxford University librarian, Ian Bowles.

I arrived at Ardfenaig House after a spectacular drive with breath-taking views along challenging single-track roads and was immediately captivated by everything I saw. To the right was a view of lochs and mountains, to the left an enchanting house smothered in pink clematis. This is a true country house, as lived in, rather than arranged in pseudo-country-house-style by a fashionable designer. There is a clutter of wellington boots, walking sticks and waterproofs in the porch, a grandfather clock in the hall and another on the landing. A graceful staircase led up past a large family portrait of two wistful small girls to my bedroom, where a low window in the very thick walls looked out over lawns and trees. There was a washbasin in the room and a plain but wholesome bathroom down a corridor. The house is full of lovely things, including many prints of Oxford, a reminder of the owner's former career. Ian Bowles cooked the excellent dinner, beginning with a great Scottish delicacy, Arbroath Smokies, served in a cheese sauce, followed by Lamb Provençale with courgettes and rice. Rhubarb fool, coffee and mints completed an enjoyable meal served at a polished table.

Ardfenaig House originally belonged to the Duke of Argyll's estate, and was used at one time as a shooting box. There has been a house on this site since the 14th century, although the present building dates from the early 18th century, with additions in the 1880s. Ian Bowles was born in Oxford and lived in France and the Far East before returning there to become a librarian. He bought the house in 1971 with a partner, Robin Drummond-Hay, former Librarian of the Queen's College, Oxford, and, as one would imagine, they filled it with a large collection of books and records. Sadly, Robin Drummond-Hay has died, but Ian Bowles continues to run Ardfenaig House successfully, kept company by a pretty little King Charles spaniel, Pennie, and helped by his fellow islanders. He is a kind, erudite and welcoming host in the best tradition of country hospitality.

At Ardfenaig House guests experience real country style in a charming home that looks over lochs and mountains. Logs are piled on the terrace, ready for warm winter fires (opposite, below left).

ARDFENAIG HOUSE, by Bunessan, Isle of Mull, Argyll PA67 6DX. **Tel.** Fionnphort (06817) 210. **Telex** No. **Owner** Ian Bowles. **Open** May to Sept. **Rooms** 3 twin, each with separate bathroom, 1 single. No showers. No TV or phone in rooms. **Facilities** Drawing room, dining room, music room, sun room, bar. 16 acres of gardens and woods with mountain and sea views. Fishing on two sea lochs, own rough shooting, sailing by arrangement. **Lunch** By arrangement. **Restrictions** Dogs by arrangement only and not in public rooms; no children under 12; no smoking in dining room. **Terms** Moderate. **Credit cards** No. **Getting there** M9 to Stirling. Exit 10 for A84 to Lochearnhead, A85 to Crainlarich, A82 to Tyndrum, A85 to Oban. Ferry to Mull ($\frac{3}{4}$-hr. crossing; cars must book). From ferry, turn L on A849 towards Fionnphort. House is 3 miles after Bunessan. NB single-track roads on Mull, allow ample time. Edinburgh to Oban 130 miles, approx 3 hrs. **Helicopter landing** Yes. **Nearest airport** Glasgow. **Nearest rail station** Oban. **Of local interest** Iona; Staffa and Fingal's Cave; beautiful scenery on Mull; birdwatching; boat trips by arrangement; Tobermory. **Whole day expeditions** Any of the above can be extended to a whole day. Take non-bookable 10 min. ferry Fishnish–Lochaline for Morvern and Ardnamurchan peninsulas. **Refreshments** Argyll Arms, Bunessan. **Dining out** Tiroran House (see p. 47).

A mansion reborn

Red deer come down from the hillside, where golden eagles nest, to browse on the lawns in the early mornings at Glenfeochan House. Owning all the land stretching down to the distant loch carries with it the responsibility of being the Laird of Kilmore, and performing certain duties, such as declaring open the local Highland Games, traditionally held on these grounds. Patricia Baber, her son James, and husband David, fell in love with this stately 1875 stone house, the turret capped with a pointed 'witch's hat' roof, the ceilings richly ornamented with plasterwork, but when they found it in April 1986, it was standing, neglected and forlorn, in a tangled wilderness of a garden amid 350 acres of wooded hills, river, pastures and loch.

In just six months of hard work they restored it to stately beauty, discovering a fine Victorian arboretum among the thickets, and specimen rhododendrons which have already won many prizes at Oban Horticultural Society shows. Wellingtonias, oak, ash, beech, hickory, maple and banks of head-high azaleas thrive; snowdrops, daffodils and bluebells carpet the ground in spring; yellow irises grow thickly on the river banks; and there are even rare wildflowers in one field that grow nowhere else in Britain. The 1½-acre walled garden is already yielding quantities of vegetables and herbs, and has a splendidly productive greenhouse where peaches and nectarines flourish. There is also a long herbaceous border well stocked with colourful flowers to cut for the house.

Trisha, who once taught at the London Cordon Bleu School, revels in the estate's supply of salmon, venison and trout, which they smoke themselves, as well as cooking in other ways (there are also shellfish in the loch). Meals are served at the long polished table in the dining room, which overlooks gardens and loch. Game soup was flavoured with juniper, thyme and mace and served with croutons; monkfish was cooked in a rich tomato and onion sauce. The tiny mange-tout peas and potatoes, as well as the raspberries and peaches for dessert were freshly gathered from the garden. I set off next day with sandwiches made from their delicious home-smoked salmon.

There is still much to look forward to: flower arranging and cooking courses are planned for the future and one day the family hopes to restore the huge ruined ballroom, where the young Princess Anne once practised Highland Reels before the Oban Ball. This is a private home, however, and you must book before arriving to stay; once here, you can be sure of a warmly hospitable reception in a spacious and splendidly restored mansion.

Local fish, fine fruits and vegetables from the hotel's river, greenhouse and garden and fresh flowers from the grounds make a feast for the eye as well as the palate.

GLENFEOCHAN HOUSE, Kilmore, by Oban, Argyll PA34 4QR. **Tel.** Kilmore (063 177) 273. **Telex** No. **Owners** David and Patricia Baber, James Petley. **Open** Feb. to Nov. **Rooms** 3 double, all with bathroom (baths only), radio, TV and electric blanket. **Facilities** Drawing room, sitting room, dining room, rod room, drying room, 350 acres of parkland, farms, hills, lochs and rivers. 5 acres of rhododendrons, azaleas and specimen trees. 1½-acre walled garden. Croquet, own rough shooting and fishing (salmon, sea trout, brown trout). **Lunch** By arrangement. **Restrictions** Dogs by arrangement only; no children under 10; no smoking in dining room. **Terms** Moderate. Reduced rates for 7 nights or longer. **Credit cards** No. **Getting there** M9 to Stirling. Exit 10 on to A84 to Lochearnhead. A85 to Crianlarich, A82 to Tyndrum, A85 to Oban. From Oban take A816 s. After 5 miles go through Kilmore; house is first L over bridge. Fork L up drive. 130 miles, approx. 3 hrs. **Helicopter landing** No. **Nearest airport** Glasgow. **Nearest rail station** Oban. **Of local interest** Oban; Arduaine Gardens, Kilmelford; Inverawe smokehouse, Taynuilt; Loch Awe; Crarae Gardens, Inverary. **Whole day expeditions** Islands of Mull and Iona; Mull of Kintyre; Seil Island; Isle of Luing; Glencoe; circuit of Loch Awe. **Refreshments** Manor House, Gallanach Road, Oban; Longhouse Buttery and Gallery, Isle of Luing; Tigh-an-Truish, Clachan-Seil; Crinan Hotel. **Dining out** Airds Hotel, Appin (see p. 43).

On the banks of Loch Awe

When Samuel Johnson and James Boswell were returning from their famous journey to the Western Isles of Scotland in October 1773, they recorded the journey south from Oban on the backs of tiny Shetland ponies to the shores of Loch Awe – a 'pretty wide lake' – over which they were ferried to continue to their destination for that night, Inverary. Today's modern road passes to the north of the loch, and the ancient route is now a single-track lane winding its way down an attractive leafy river valley, through the tiny village of Kilchrenan, to what was once the ferry inn and is now the Taychreggan Hotel.

Standing on the wooded shores of one of Scotland's most beautiful lochs, the hotel, which is built around a cobbled courtyard, embodies all the charms of past centuries. The stone-flagged entrance hall leads to low-ceilinged sitting rooms which look out over the loch through massively thick walls; many of the bedrooms have dormer windows and all are furnished with antiques, maps and prints. This sense of the past is combined with a thoroughly modern Scandinavian atmosphere created by Tove Taylor, the owner's Danish wife. She has installed double glazing, pine staircases and bedheads and a splendid iron stove in the sitting room; the whitewashed brickwalled dining room is decorated with blue Copenhagen china and woven wall sculptures. An amazingly generous 'koldt bord' selection of seafoods and salads is offered here at lunchtime, and in the evenings the simple dinner of local produce is served by candlelight. Lunchtime snacks are served in the bar, where guests can relax in easychairs and read the books or admire the framed fishing flies, record-breaking salmon or models of fishing boats. The bedrooms are decorated with antiques and Laura Ashley sprigged fabrics and wallpapers; the beds are well-sprung, the good bathrooms have showers and everything is kept in immaculate order by a team of smiling Scottish and Danish girls.

The house is surrounded by pleasant informal gardens with azaleas, mown paths and benches on which to sit and enjoy the superb view. There are boats if you wish to do some fishing, and enchanting walks beside the loch where you may glimpse, as I did, red deer in the early evening. John Taylor is that rare and priceless treasure, a thoroughly professional owner who devotes all his energies to making his guests comfortable, be they baronets or businessmen, honeymooning couples or lone walkers, families or foreign visitors. All are welcomed with equal warmth, all repeatedly return to this ideal historic hideaway.

This solidly built inn, with enchanting views, is the ideal retreat in which to relax by a beautiful loch (opposite), and a perfect centre for hikers and anglers. Above is the one that didn't get away!

TAYCHREGGAN HOTEL, Kilchrenan, by Taynuilt, Argyll PA35 IHQ. **Tel.** Kilchrenan (08663) 211. **Telex** No. **Owners** John and Tove Taylor. **Open** Easter to mid-Oct. **Rooms** 1 suite, 14 double, 2 single, all with bathroom (including wall shower), radio, baby listening and direct-dial phone. No TV in rooms. **Facilities** 2 lounges, lounge-hall, TV/quiet room, restaurant, bar, 25-acre lochside garden, loch and mountain views. Shooting, stalking, riding, fishing, sailing and wind-surfing by arrangement. 4 boats and engines. **Lunch** Yes. **Restrictions** None. **Terms** Medium. **Credit cards** Access/Amex/Diners/Visa. **Getting there** M9 to Stirling. Exit 10 on to A84 to Lochearnhead. A85 to Crianlarich, A82 to Tyndrum, A85 (Oban road). Just before Taynuilt, turn L on to B845 through Kilchrenan down to Taychreggan on loch side. 118 miles, approx. 3 hrs. **Helicopter landing** Yes. **Nearest airport** Glasgow (local airfield at Oban). **Nearest rail station** Taynuilt. **Of local interest** Inverary Castle; Ardanaiseig Garden; Cruachan Dam; Glencoe; standing stones at Kilmartin; Inverawe smoke-house. **Whole day expeditions** Islands of Mull, Luing, Iona and Staffa (Fingal's Cave); Fort William; gardens at Arduaine, Crarae, Achnacloich. **Refreshments** Long-house Buttery and Gallery, Isle of Luing; Holly Tree, Appin; Creggans Inn, Strachur; Crinan Hotel, Crinan. **Dining out** Inverlochy Castle (see p. 33); Airds Hotel, Appin (see p. 43).

Continental charm

The busy little town of Callander, set amid spectacularly lovely lochs and hills, attracts many tourists and walkers. The Romans built an army camp here, and the town's history goes back to the Druids, who celebrated the summer solstice on a nearby mountaintop. Always a natural stopping place for travellers to the west coast, a military road and a stage-coach route once passed through. The Victorians loved the town, and built the elaborate summer villas that still remain, as do their postboxes marked V.R.

Turning sharply off Main Street between two pink houses, I followed a long drive through twenty acres of leafy woodland, before passing through fine wrought-iron gates into beautifully kept gardens with manicured lawns and clipped box and yew trees. Roman Camp Hotel stands in a bend of the River Teith, its grey slate roof and pointed turrets making it look like a miniature French château. Built in 1625 as a hunting lodge for the Dukes of Perth, it is painted bright strawberry-icecream pink, a local sign, during the Jacobite uprising, of a sympathizer with Bonnie Prince Charlie. An ancient, massive door, studded with hand-made nails, opens into a small hall lined with linenfold panelling, where a cheerful log fire burns in the vast grate. There was an efficient, friendly girl at the desk and my bag was swiftly taken upstairs. The Belgian wife of former owner Lord Esher furnished the house with painted furniture, a tradition maintained by the present owners, so the wardrobe in my bedroom was green with gold flourishes. The fireplace was delightfully ornate and there were fresh flowers and a courtesy tea-tray with newly-baked shortbread. Small windows provided a view of the river, where I later saw a kingfisher, and my well-equipped bathroom looked out over flowering Japanese cherry trees to distant hills.

Downstairs a low-ceilinged bar led unexpectedly to a large gracious drawing room decorated with antique silk brocade wallpaper. The book-lined library, which has an elaborate Edwardian ceiling and a tiny turret chapel, was hung with a fine collection of the works of modern Scottish artists. Another surprise was the dining room, totally modern, but with ceiling rafters painted to resemble those of 17th-century Scottish mansions. The food was delicious, and included local fresh asparagus, crayfish and strawberries. In the morning, the freshly baked bread, croissants and brioche reminded me that Swiss chef-owner Sami Denzler first trained as a chef-pâtissier. Mrs Denzler, half-Irish, half-Scottish, now quietly and efficiently manages the hotel. Historically fascinating, gastronomically polished, and a perfect setting: what more could one ask of any hotel?

Painted furniture is a distinctive feature of the hotel (above). Formal gardens, panelling and decorative plaster ceilings create an atmosphere of old-world luxury (opposite and overleaf).

ROMAN CAMP HOTEL, Callander, Perthshire FK17 8BG. **Tel.** Callander (0877) 30003. **Telex** No. **Owners** Mr and Mrs Sami Denzler. **Open** Mid-March to mid-Nov. **Rooms** 3 suites, 11 double, all with bathroom (incl. showers, mostly wall-mounted), direct-dial phone, TV, radio and hairdrier. **Facilities** Lounge, lounge-hall, library, sun lounge, dining room, facilities for small meetings. 20-acre grounds and gardens with own river fishing. **Lunch** By arrangement only. **Restrictions** Dogs by arrangement only and not in public rooms; no smoking in dining room. **Terms** Moderate. Some reduced rates March to April and Nov. **Credit cards** No. **Getting there** M9 towards Stirling. Exit 10 for A84 to Callander. Turn L in Main Street. 52 miles, approx. 1 hr. **Helicopter landing** Yes, by arrangement. **Nearest airport** Edinburgh. **Nearest rail station** Stirling. **Of local interest** Callander (shopping for woollens); Stirling (town and castle); Doune Castle and motor museum; Lake of Menteith and ruined priory of Inchmahome; Loch Katrine (sailing); Balquhidder (Rob Roy's grave). **Whole day expeditions** Tours of Trossach mountains; Burrell Collection and galleries and museums of Glasgow; Scone Palace, Perth; golf at Callander, Gleneagles and St Andrews. **Refreshments** Tea shops in Callander. **Dining out** Cromlix House, Dunblane (see p. 59).

Old-world splendour

Rabbits browsing on the wide grass verges scattered for cover as I drove up the long approach to Cromlix House one evening, though a magnificent cock pheasant strolling among the hundreds of yellow daffodils on the lawns in front of the house totally ignored my arrival. A massive stone entrance porch leads to a large panelled hall, where I found a fire burning brightly in a hearth flanked by brass-studded leather armchairs. Candles illumined majestic stags' heads on the walls, which looked down on enormous bowls of beautifully arranged spring flowers and a large antique table with a guest book invitingly open. A friendly girl instantly appeared, and I was shown up to the Orchid Room, where I was to stay.

This is a very imposing house, built in 1880 to entertain guests at lavish shooting parties (Edward VII stayed here in 1908). The two main suites have a turret at each corner and the furniture made for them still in place. One retains an original Victorian bathroom, with incredibly complicated but extremely efficient plumbing; each has a large comfortable sitting room. My room was more modest, but still vast, with a sizeable pot of orchids, easy chairs upholstered in green velvet and a wardrobe large enough to hold a month's clothes. The dressing table had an antique mirror, the walls were pale pink and the attractive curtains were patterned with exotic birds and bamboo. The bathroom was of similar size: the bath was lost in one corner.

Before dinner there was an opportunity to enjoy the views from the immense drawing room, which looks out over a 5000-acre estate that ensures privacy and quiet. Apéritifs were offered with miniature freshly baked wild mushroom vol-au-vents, sesame-seed pastries and slivers of rye bread with smoked salmon, while the manager came round to discuss the menu with each guest. The candlelit meal began with asparagus soup, followed by fresh halibut. Chicken flavoured with mace was accompanied by home-made pasta, green beans and a side salad. The dessert, fresh strawberries in an almond tuile with kirsch icecream, was delicious; coffee and handmade chocolates were served afterwards in the drawing room. Breakfast is excellent, and those not wishing to join the communal table may order a tray upstairs.

Guests may stroll over to fish the nearby loch or on inclement days enjoy the flower-filled conservatory or book-lined library (the family chapel should not be missed). The staff are discreetly invisible unless required and the house has retained the atmosphere of a family home; its owner still lives nearby and can often be met strolling through the grounds. Cromlix House vividly evokes the splendour of bygone days.

An exterior view of the Victorian conservatory, imposing turrets and family chapel at Cromlix House (above). Guests enjoy the sunny drawing room, comfortable bedrooms furnished with antiques, the fine food and excellent choice of whiskies (opposite and overleaf).

CROMLIX HOUSE, Cromlix, Dunblane, Perthshire FK15 9JT. **Tel.** Dunblane (0786) 822125. **Telex** 77959 CLX HSE G. **Owner** The Hon. Ronald J. Eden. **Manager** Grant Howlett. **Open** All year. **Rooms** 14 double, 8 with own sitting room, all with bathroom (12 with wall-mounted shower), radio, TV and direct-dial phone. **Facilities** Sitting room, 2 dining rooms, conservatory, library, boardroom, private chapel, 5000-acre estate with 4 lochs, river, woods and moors. Own shooting and loch fishing; horse riding by arrangement. **Lunch** Available daily, but by arrangement only. **Restrictions** No smoking in dining rooms. **Terms** Expensive. Some winter breaks at reduced rates. **Credit cards** Access/Amex/Diners/Visa. **Getting there** M9/A9 to Dunblane, then L on B8033 through Kinbuck. 40 miles, approx. 1 hr. **Helicopter landing** Yes. **Nearest airport** Edinburgh. **Nearest rail station** Dunblane. **Of local interest** Stirling and Doune Castles; Dunblane Cathedral and museum; Edinburgh; Burrell Collection, Glasgow; golf at Gleneagles. **Whole day expeditions** Tours of the Trossach mountains; Loch Lomond; Perth. **Refreshments** Broughton's, Doune; Sheriffmuir Inn, Sheriffmuir; The Heritage, Stirling. **Dining out** Eagle's Nest, Gleneagles (see p. 63); Peat Inn (see p. 73); La Potiniere, Gullane; Kippling's, Bridge of Allan.

International fame

It is hard to imagine anyone feeling bored at Gleneagles. Here at last for those accompanying the dedicated golfer is an arcade of luxury boutiques, a sport and leisure complex with heated indoor landscaped pool and children's pool, with its own poolside restaurant, jacuzzi, solarium, sauna, hot tub, squash, table tennis, billiards, exercise gym and beauty salon. There is a tennis programme organized by Wimbledon champion Virginia Wade, a shooting programme organized by Jackie Stewart (grandson of a gamekeeper as well as former British champion shot and world champion racing driver) and a horse-riding programme organized by Captain Mark Phillips, husband of the Princess Royal. Pheasant, duck and rough shooting, stalking, salmon and trout fishing are organized in the appropriate season. However, it is of course for its golf that Gleneagles has always been most famous. There are four impeccably maintained courses, a world-class golfer always on hand to coach, a pro shop, and Dormy House restaurant and bar out amid the greens. Private houses in the grounds allow their owners a year-round country-club existence amid incomparable scenery.

Gleneagles was one of the great fashionable railway hotels built in the 1920s and has now happily been gloriously restored to its former magnificence. More than nine million pounds have been spent to give yesterday's splendour today's comfort. I drove up to the door to be warmly greeted by an enormous Highlander wearing the kilt. This was Jock the Linkman, who summoned a porter for me, and parked my car. The vast hall was immaculate, with a spectacular arrangement of fresh flowers and the desk staff were welcoming and efficient. My luxuriously comfortable room, with kingsize bed and marble

bathroom, had chinoiserie decor and black lacquer furniture. Miniature suites with curtained four-poster beds are tucked up under the eaves on the top floor; less vast than many other of the rooms, they are much in demand by honeymooners, I was told. Public rooms are huge and well-furnished, luscious old-fashioned cream teas are served in the afternoon, service is swift and polite, views spectacular. The main restaurant serves Highland beef, game and fish, while the Eagle's Nest restaurant specializes in gourmet dishes.

For visitors who wish to experience a nostalgic return to the grandeur of the past, while enjoying all a modern international hotel has to offer, Gleneagles reigns supreme in Scotland.

Brilliant flowers and splendid views are a welcoming sight at the entrance of Gleneagles. Jock the Linkman (opposite, top right) is the first to greet guests, park cars and summon porters. Overleaf: decor is to international standards of style and luxury; the four-poster suites are popular with honeymooners.

THE GLENEAGLES HOTEL, Auchterarder, Perthshire PH3 1NF. **Tel.** Auchterarder (0764) 62231. **Telex** 76105. **Owners** Guinness plc. **Managing Director and General Manager** Peter J. Lederer. **Rooms** 20 suites, 186 double, 48 single, all with bathroom (including wall shower), radio, TV, direct-dial phone, mini-bar, in-house videos. **Facilities** Drawing room with 24-hr service, library, 4 restaurants, 3 bars, 8 conference/banqueting rooms, 750-acre grounds, 4 golf courses, indoor pool, children's pool, 3 tables for billiards and snooker, croquet, putting, table tennis, squash, jogging track with map, gym, hot tubs, jacuzzi, sauna, solaria, massage, beauty shop. Own riding, shooting, tennis, loch and river fishing and sailing; pro golf, squash and shooting. Clothes shops, news-stand and tobacconist, bank, post office. **Lunch** Yes. **Restrictions** Pets by prior arrangement only. **Terms** Medium. Some special all-inclusive breaks. **Credit cards** All major cards. **Getting there** M9, A9 through Stirling and Dunblane. L at hotel signs. 50 miles, approx. 1 hr. **Helicopter landing** Yes. **Nearest airport** Edinburgh. **Nearest rail station** Gleneagles. **Of local interest** Whisky distilleries and woollen mills; Strathallan Air Museum; Caithness Glass and Crystal Works; Perth; Stirling; Auchterarder. **Whole day expeditions** Edinburgh; Glasgow (Burrell Collection); Trossachs; Pitlochry Festival Theatre; Royal Deeside; Inverness and Loch Ness. **Refreshments/Dining out** Consult Hall Porter.

Simple excellence

Hanging in the hall of the Old Mansion House Hotel at Auchterhouse near Dundee is an account of the building's history that goes back to 1245. The ruined Wallace Tower still survives from the original moated castle, although it is now a clematis-smothered feature of the well-tended gardens, which are resplendent in early autumn with herbaceous borders worthy of the Chelsea Flower Show. They slope down to a watergarden beside what was once the moat and is now a cheerful small brook; nearby is a large walled vegetable garden which provides fresh produce for the restaurant.

The tall impressive whitewashed building is entered through the massive undercroft, built in the 15th century. This is a low arched stone chamber, filled with flowers, from where a flight of stone steps – this is not a hotel for the unfit – leads up to the hall, which has one of the finest Jacobean plasterwork ceilings in Scotland. Owner Nigel Bell and his wife Eva explained to me that they intended to concentrate on the restaurant when they bought and restored the castle in 1978. It was an instant success, and people drove out from Dundee for snacks in the courtyard bar or meals in the elegantly formal dining room overlooking the gardens, which has an elaborately carved overmantel as well as another magnificent 17th-century plasterwork ceiling. I much enjoyed a melon and shrimp cocktail with home-made mayonnaise, tender roast beef, Yorkshire pudding and garden vegetables. Like the apple and raspberry tart with thick cream which followed, they had the fresh tastiness of the very best home cooking. There is also a more sophisticated *à la carte* menu offering Scottish specialities – or indeed any dish you would like, given enough warning.

Having eaten so well, business guests wished to return with their wives and families for holidays, so the Bells furnished six bedrooms with simple comforts. One has a four poster, wildly sloping floor and a turret garderobe and two have charmingly naive Elizabethan plasterwork ceilings. Two smaller rooms at the back look out into the branches of a huge lime tree and there is a vast attic bedroom from which you can peer straight into the housemartins' nests under the eaves. There are duvets, modern bathrooms, phones, mini-bars and ample hanging space, though certainly no designer decor. The success with which the comforts of a welcoming hotel have been combined with the atmosphere and charm of an ancient castle can be judged by the fact that the Bells have never had to advertise and that guests return yearly from as far away as Australia and San Francisco.

Visitors warm to the blazing fire in the sitting room (opposite): note the fine plaster ceiling. Brilliant autumn flowers are a feature of the well tended gardens (above).

THE OLD MANSION HOUSE HOTEL, Auchterhouse, by Dundee DD3 0QN. **Tel.** Auchterhouse (082626) 366. **Telex** No. **Owners** Nigel and Eva Bell. **Manager** Edward Murphy. **Open** 5 Jan to 24 Dec. **Rooms** 1 suite, 5 double, all with bathroom (5 with bath, 1 with wall shower), radio, TV, direct-dial phone, mini-bar. **Facilities** Dining room, private dining room, courtyard bar, residents' bar and library. 10 acres of gardens with heated outdoor pool, squash and tennis courts, croquet, brook and woodland. **Lunch** Yes. **Restrictions** Children welcome in dining room for lunch but not for dinner. **Terms** Moderate. Reduced weekend rate for 2 people staying 2 nights. **Credit cards** All major cards. **Getting there** A90 over Forth Bridge, M90 to Perth, A85 to Dundee, A923 to Muirhead, R on B954 after 2 miles, hotel on left. 55 miles, approx. 1¼ hrs. **Helicopter landing** Yes. **Nearest airport** Edinburgh or Dundee. **Nearest rail station** Dundee. **Of local interest** Dundee; Glamis Castle; Perth; golf at Gleneagles, Carnoustie and St Andrews. **Whole day expeditions** Aberdeen; Grampian Mountains. **Refreshments** None nearby. **Dining out** Peat Inn (see p. 73).

A golfer's dream

To play the challenging Old Course at St Andrews must surely be the ambition of every keen golfer visiting Scotland. Even for non-players, the ancient university city has enormous charm. It was therefore with delight that I discovered that Trusthouse Forte, who run Brown's Hotel and the Hyde Park Hotel in London so successfully, had just completed renovating at the cost of many millions the delightful Rusack's hotel, which overlooks the Old Course 18th green. A lavish product of the great years of the railways, built in the late 19th century, it had fallen into sad decline by the mid-1970s. After a period of considerable improvements, it has been rescued and redecorated with flair and panache.

A promenade lined with mirrors and elegant settees runs right through the hotel, from the pillared, high-ceilinged, cherry-coloured entrance hall at one end, furnished with vast oil paintings, antiques and comfortable chairs, to the library at the other. Next to the library is a glass-fronted lounge with views over the Old Course to the Club House, long sandy beaches and the sea beyond. A polished *maître d'hôtel* presides over the restaurant, which is entirely lined with dark green and maroon paisley fabric and has stiffly starched white damask cloths on the tables. The excellent and varied menu is of a standard equal to the better London hotels, service is swift and attentive, the bread is freshly baked, and I can recommend the comprehensive and delicious breakfasts. In addition, refreshments and snacks are available all day in the club-like golfers' bar and in the upstairs lounge.

Striking colour schemes have been used in the fifty bedrooms and in the Royal Suite, which commemorates a stay by the Prince of Wales at the turn of the century. Single rooms are decorated mainly in

dark blue and white, with bold and intricate matching wallpaper and curtains. Double rooms display a slightly startling use of dark green walls with maroon and blue curtains. My own room was delightful. The coved ceiling was very high and the walls were painted pale apricot to match the floral glazed chintz bedcover and curtains of deeper peach with jade and white. There was a plate of fruit, with napkin, knife and finger bowl, and a direct-dial telephone. The ample hanging space was perfumed with a lavender bag and an extremely comprehensive courtesy teatray complemented the very rapid room service. Furniture is good reproduction antique, including the fixtures in the bathrooms, which are also supplied with generous toiletries, plenty of towels and excellent showers. All the staff were particularly welcoming. This is a most happy blend of grandeur recreated and modern comforts.

Rusacks is a grand railway hotel of the 1890s (left), with colourfully and individually decorated rooms (above). Overleaf: The reception rooms are filled with books, paintings and antiques, with views over the 18th Hole of the world-famous golf course.

RUSACK'S, Pilmour Links, St Andrews, Fife KY16 9JQ. **Tel.** St Andrews (0334) 74321. **Telex** No. **Owners** Trusthouse Forte. **General Manager** Eric Brown. **Open** All year. **Rooms** 2 suites, 41 double or twin, 7 single, all with bathroom (with wall shower), direct-dial phone, radio and TV. **Facilities** Sun lounge, dining room, golfers' bar, promenade sitting room, laundry, drycleaning, photocopying, typing, shoe cleaning and picnic hamper services. Safe. Views over Old Course to sea and sandy public beach. **Lunch** Yes. **Restrictions** None. **Terms** Medium. Reduced rates for Christmas and other breaks; special conference terms. **Credit cards** All major cards. **Getting there** A90 over Forth Bridge, M90. Exit 8 for A91 to St Andrews. Head for sea and golf course; hotel is beside 18th green. 50 miles, approx. 1 hr. **Helicopter landing** No. **Nearest airport** Edinburgh. **Nearest rail station** Cupar. **Of local interest** St Andrews (golf, university, old town); countryside of Fife; Dundee; golf at Carnoustie. **Whole day expeditions** Perth; Scone Palace; Grampian mountains; Edinburgh. **Refreshments** Many small restaurants in St Andrews. **Dining out** Old Mansion House, Auchterhouse (see p. 67); Peat Inn (see p. 73).

Home of a celebrated chef

David Wilson, chef-patron of the Peat Inn, is a square, bearded, friendly Scotsman from Glasgow. Until his late twenties he was a marketing executive with a big international concern, living in England, and visiting France often to enjoy the creative cooking of Michelin-starred restaurants. But he was not happy with his career. With great courage, he and his wife, Patricia, decided that the most important thing in life was to do what they enjoyed. David left his secure job, worked for two years in a friend's restaurant, and then bought the Peat Inn, which they opened in November 1972, just as Patricia was expecting the arrival at any moment of their second child. Happy to be back in their native Scotland, with its superb fish and game, they worked hard while raising their family, and established an international reputation for outstanding cooking which won for David the accolade of a Michelin star, very rare for a British chef.

Together the Wilsons have transformed this ancient little drovers' inn on the route from Cupar to St Andrews. Recently they have added eight very comfortable bedrooms in the same attractive and welcoming style as the Inn. Patricia, a graduate in textile design from Glasgow Art College, has much enjoyed decorating them with high quality Osborne & Little fabrics. For furniture they returned to France, bringing back delightful French provincial pieces. Bathrooms are marble, well-equipped, and have good showers.

Walk through the front door of the Peat Inn and you will find yourself in a low-ceilinged beamed room, with a fire burning cheerfully on a raised hearth. There are groups of comfortable settees, Victorian chaise-longues and chairs, where one sits

while reading the menu and ordering. The restaurant itself is in three rooms, two small ones opening off the passage which runs the length of the inn, and a larger room at the back, tapestry-hung, candle-lit at night, with arched windows looking out over fields and woods. I decided on the gourmet 'tasting' menu, small portions of six courses. Lobster and crab in a citrus vinaigrette was followed by gratin of Arbroath Smokie and smoked salmon, scallops, pigeon breast in a red wine sauce fragrant with juniper berries, some perfect brie, and a platter of sorbets and sliced fresh fruits so artistically arranged I thought at first they had been painted on the plate. Petits fours and coffee were delicious. The vast, reasonably priced wine list, which covers many countries, has excellent clarets and burgundies, including half bottles and interesting vintages.

The village in which the inn stands is so small that it is simply called Peat Inn. Thanks to the Wilsons, it is now marked on every gourmet's map of Britain.

Michelin-starred chef David Wilson creates culinary works of art (opposite, below), served in the simple oak-beamed dining room (above). The reception rooms are perfectly in tune with the inn's quiet country style (opposite, above).

THE PEAT INN, Peat Inn by Cupar, Fife KY15 5LH. **Tel.** Peat Inn (033 484) 206. **Telex** No. **Owners** David and Patricia Wilson. **Open** All year, except every Sunday and Monday, 2 weeks in Jan. and a week in both March and Oct. **Rooms** 8 suites, all with bathroom (incl. fixed shower and bath), TV, direct-dial phone, radio. (1 room is on ground floor, avoiding the use of stairs.) **Facilities** Sitting room, restaurant, small garden. Golf at St Andrews can be arranged. **Lunch** Yes (must book). **Restrictions** No dogs; no children under 10; no smoking in restaurant. **Terms** Medium. **Credit cards** Access/Amex/Diners/Visa. **Getting there** A9 over Forth Bridge, M90 to Exit 8. A91

towards St Andrews, turning off to Peat Inn about 5 miles before St Andrews. 45 miles, approx. 1 hr. **Helicopter landing** No. **Nearest airport** Edinburgh. **Nearest rail station** Cupar. **Of local interest** Ancient university town of St Andrews; Hill of Tarvit House; Falkland Palace; Earlshall Castle and gardens; Kellie Castle; coast. **Whole day expeditions** Edinburgh; Glamis Castle; Scone Palace; Perth. **Refreshments** Many small restaurants in St Andrews and coastal fishing villages. **Dining out** Rusack's, St Andrews (see p. 69); Cellar Restaurant, Anstruther; Ostler's Close Restaurant, Cupar.

A sophisticated delight

Aficionados of Blake's Hotel in London will enjoy the decor of One, Devonshire Gardens for it was in part inspired by that of Anouska Hempel Weinberg's deliciously extravagant and fanciful fashionable retreat. Dark greeny-blue walls and ceilings in the pillared hall, staircase and dining room give way to pale colours in the huge high-ceilinged drawing room, which has comfortable couches, tall green silk plants and plenty of magazines. Drinks are set out here in the evening and served by one of the polite, unobtrusive staff. Starched white cloths and fresh flowers, gleaming silverware and crystal brighten the dining-room, which has a short but good menu.

Of the eight bedrooms, four are decorated in sombre tones, four in light. My bedroom was at the top of the house – there is no elevator, the unathletic must be warned. On one landing I was startled by a life-size model of a seated man which turned out to be a work of modern art. The bedroom walls were the same colour as the hall and the ceiling sloped sharply. The specially-made six-foot-wide four-poster was draped with heavy flounced curtains, and a colour television was discreetly hidden in the skirts of a draped circular table. The walk-in clothes closet was huge and the elegant bathroom, decorated with 18th-century prints, had an antique-style panelled bath with gilded taps and hand-shower, and masses of fluffy white towels. A bowl of vivid green apples was on the table together with a generous scattering of fashion magazines. A helpful booklet offered same-day dry cleaning and laundry, assistance with shopping, advice on places to eat, suggestions for touring and willingness to make on-going travel arrangements by hire-car or helicopter, plane or train. The mutter of traffic from the nearby main road was barely audible, and quietened during the night.

One, Devonshire Gardens is the first house in an elegant terrace leading off a broad, tree-lined thoroughfare in a fashionable residential area of Glasgow. The Botanic Gardens are close by and Glasgow's splendid Burrell Collection is only a short drive away. This pleasantly civilized and elegant small hotel is sometimes taken over completely by some noted personage and his or her entourage, who enjoy the comfort and privacy of its large rooms. At other times it can provide a most pleasant base, as I myself found, for the lone traveller in a large city whose magnificent galleries and museums are too often neglected by visitors to Scotland.

Supremely stylish interiors at One, Devonshire Gardens begin with the midnight blue staircase and dining room (above and opposite). Overleaf: A lavishly draped four-poster bed; fluffy white towels are piled on an antique rail by a stained-glass casement window.

ONE, DEVONSHIRE GARDENS, Glasgow G12 0UX. **Tel.** Glasgow (041) 339 2001. **Telex** No. **Owner** Kenneth McCulloch. **Managers** Jim Kerr and Ms Alison Kerr. **Open** All year. **Rooms** 8 double, all with bathroom (7 with bath and hand shower, 1 with wall shower and no bath), direct-dial phone and TV. **Facilities** Drawing room, dining room. **Restrictions** Dogs by arrangement only. **Terms** Medium. **Credit cards** Access/Amex/Diners/Visa. **Getting there** M8. 46 miles, approx. ¾ hr. Ask hotel for exact instructions. **Helicopter landing** No. **Nearest airport** Glasgow.

Nearest rail station Glasgow. **Of local interest** Glasgow Cathedral; Burrell Collection; Kelvingrove Art Galleries and Museum; Hunterian Museum; buildings by Charles Rennie Mackintosh, including Glasgow School of Art and church at Queen's Cross; Loch Lomond. **Whole day expeditions** Edinburgh; Trossachs; Culzean Castle (see p. 87). **Refreshments/Dining out** Consult the hotel staff, as the reputations of local restaurants fluctuate rapidly.

A gracious experience

Humphrey and Rozi Spurway were advised that the best thing to do with the neglected Georgian mansion in the middle of their 3000-acre sporting estate was to pull it down. Daylight came in through the rafters and the surrounding formal gardens had become a jungle. Undaunted, they determined instead to bring it back to all its original 1807 elegance and after two years spent on extensive restoration this is what they have triumphantly achieved. Harburn House now provides perfect accommodation for a shooting party, small conference, or guests who choose to bring their own staff and friends to take over the entire house for a week or a month. It is also ideal for private visitors to Scotland wanting to stay in peaceful countryside near Edinburgh and desiring more individual attention than a hotel would offer. They will enjoy being thoroughly pampered and deliciously fed by the chef and house staff, and joined at dinner if they wish by the Spurways.

The house has never lost the atmosphere of a private home. Its pillared entrance hall has a graceful staircase spiralling upwards to the bedrooms and downwards to the dining room. The spacious drawing room, furnished in soft apricots, creams and browns, has a sparkling crystal chandelier and a wide bay window overlooking a series of lakes whose construction has been a recent project, like the restoration of the walled garden. A heroic lifesized oil painting by Raeburn of an ancestor, Sir David Baird, commemorating the battle of Seringapatam in India, dominates the billiard room, whose match-sized table has a custom-made wooden top for conferences and handsome hide and oak chairs. There is a small classical library and a sunny sitting room which overlooks the smooth green croquet lawn, magnificent rhododendrons and well-wooded parkland with grazing sheep at the front of the house.

I enjoyed chatting to Rozi Spurway as we dined excellently at a long polished table. Fresh salmon roulade was followed by roast duck with a redcurrant and orange sauce, mange-tout peas, tomatoes stuffed with leeks and mushrooms lightly flavoured with basil. Dessert was a featherlight puff-pastry case filled with double cream and summer fruits grown on the estate. Each bedroom is different: the largest are furnished with antique four-poster beds, those in the attic have sloping ceilings and a former nursery is still decorated with its original 19th-century prints for children. All are equipped with excellent modern bathrooms and decorated with fresh, elegant chintzes. A visit to Harburn House is a thoroughly gracious experience, which – since this is a private house – must be arranged well in advance.

The elegant Regency proportions of Harburn House are set in extensive grounds (opposite). One of the comfortably furnished four-poster bedrooms is shown above.

HARBURN HOUSE, Harburn, West Calder, Mid-Lothian EH55 8RN. **Tel.** Harburn (0506) 410742/872986. **Telex** 776242 CIRCLE G. **Owners** Humphrey and Rozi Spurway. **Open** All year. **Rooms** 8 double, 7 with bathroom (2 with wall shower), all with radio and direct-dial phone; 4 more double bedrooms in Loch Lodge. **Facilities** Drawing room, sitting room, library, billiard and conference room, dining room, private sporting estate of 3000 acres (with gardens, lochs, woods, etc.), own shooting, stalking and fishing in lochs and river (salmon and trout). Shooting rights extend over another 22,000 acres. Putting, croquet, billiards, tennis, riding, golf. Sea fishing by arrangement. **Lunch** By arrangement. **Restrictions** Dogs by arrangement only. **Terms** Medium. Some seasonal reductions Feb. to April; reductions for groups. **Credit cards** Access/Amex/Diners/Visa. **Getting there** M8, Exit 1 to Livingston. Follow dual carriageway and turn R on A71 to Kilmarknock. At West Calder, turn L at garage on to Harburn Road. After 2 miles, turn L at golf course; entrance to house is 250 yds on R. 14 miles, approx. $\frac{1}{2}$ hr. **Helicopter landing** Yes. **Nearest airport/Nearest rail station** Edinburgh (courtesy car will collect by arrangement). **Of local interest** Edinburgh; Burrell Collection, Glasgow; Hopetoun House; Dalmeny House. **Whole day expeditions** Loch Lomond; Stirling; Perth; Trossachs; Sir Walter Scott's Border Country; Burns Country. **Refreshments** Nothing nearby. **Dining out** Houston House, Uphall; many Edinburgh restaurants.

Luxury, Edinburgh

In 1894 horsedrawn carriages brought the first travellers to the Caledonian Railway Company's newly opened Prince's Street Station, clip-clopping under the left of three arches in the elaborate red sandstone facade. Foot passengers entered the vast booking hall through the middle arch, the station's very grand restaurant was on the right and seven tracks brought the mighty steam engines puffing into the heart of the city. Nine years later, on 21 December 1903, after over fifty years of hopes raised and dashed by the fluctuating fortunes of the railways, the Company at last opened the Caledonian Hotel adjacent to the station. Even for those lavish times the magnificence of its glittering marble splendour was breathtaking: its telegraphic address was LUXURY, EDINBURGH.

During the gilded 1920s and 30s the hotel played host to kings and maharajahs, film stars and millionaires. The 1950s and 60s saw visits from the king and queen of Nepal, Marlene Dietrich, Bob Hope and Bing Crosby. After Prince's Street Station closed in 1965, the hotel slipped into shabby dilapidation, from which it was triumphantly rescued by the Gleneagles Company in 1981. Over five million pounds went to clean the grime from the red sandstone exterior, double-glaze all the windows, and refurbish, replumb and redecorate the interior. The chef installed in the newly resplendent Pompadour Restaurant was promptly awarded the title of best Scottish chef of the year.

As you arrive, attentive porters meet you and will park your car for you behind the hotel as your luggage is whisked away. The entrance hall gleams with marble. There are elevators, an imposing main staircase, a news-stand and comfortable, elegant seating areas. In the lounges and Gazebo Restaurant you can be served light meals and afternoon tea. Bedrooms and bathrooms are enormous and well-modernized, with efficient showers and plenty of space for luggage and clothes. From my bedroom, pleasantly furnished in pale yellow, jade and cerise, with soft down pillows on the bed, I had a breathtaking view over the craggy grassy slopes that ascend to Edinburgh Castle.

Norfolk Capital Hotels, which now owns the Caledonian, has already invested a further million, refurbishing bedrooms and adding a Presidential and six other suites. This is a well-run, convenient luxury hotel of international status in one of Britain's most beautiful cities. With Prince's Street on its doorstep for last-minute shopping, it is the ideal place to begin or finish a visit to Scotland.

The glittering floodlit facade (above), the magnificent views over Edinburgh Castle (opposite, above) and the traditional elegance of the dining room (opposite, below) are memorable features.

THE CALEDONIAN HOTEL, Princes Street, Edinburgh, Lothian EH1 2AB. **Tel.** Edinburgh (031) 225 2433. **Telex** 72179 CALEY. **Owners** Norfolk Capital Hotels. **General Manager** Dermot Fitzpatrick. **Open** All year. **Rooms** 24 suites, 176 double, 38 single, all with bathroom (with wall shower), direct-dial phone, radio, TV, minibars, most with trouser press. Some rooms are reserved for non-smokers, ladies travelling alone and the disabled. **Facilities** Lounge, 2 restaurants, 3 bars, conference and meeting rooms, small garden. Room service, valet and same-day laundry, pressing and dry-cleaning. News-stand and gift shop, ladies' and gentlemen's hairdressing, jogging map for Princes Street Gardens. Parking for 150 cars. **Lunch** Yes. **Restrictions** No dogs. **Terms** Medium. Reduced rates for groups. **Credit cards** Access/Amex/Carte Blanche/Diners/Visa. **Getting there** 5 mins. by taxi from Waverley train station; 20 mins. by taxi from Edinburgh airport. **Helicopter landing** No. **Nearest airport** Edinburgh. **Nearest rail station** Edinburgh (Waverley). **Of local interest** Edinburgh Castle; Holyrood Palace; National Gallery of Scotland; National Portrait Gallery of Scotland; Royal Mile; St Giles's Cathedral; Georgian streets and squares of the New Town, especially the National Trust for Scotland's Georgian house in Charlotte Square; shopping in Princes Street; Botanic Gardens; Dalmeny House and church; Hopetoun House; international arts festival every August. **Whole day expeditions** Sir Walter Scott's Border Country; Glasgow (especially Burrell Collection); Scone Palace, Perth; golf at St Andrews, Muirfield and Gleneagles. **Refreshments/Dining out** Consult the hotel's porters, as city restaurants rise and fall fast.

Edwardian elegance

Set in countryside made famous by Sir Walter Scott, Greywalls is a beautiful Sir Edwin Lutyens mansion built in 1901 on the edge of the famous Muirfield golf course. Like many of this noted Edwardian architect's houses, it has great personality, a wonderfully welcoming atmosphere and a garden designed by Gertrude Jekyll. Lutyens wrote that a home should be 'first and foremost a refuge, which must have a sense of enclosure, a sense of security and a feeling of strength'. He could have been describing Greywalls.

Passing through the entrance gate, visitors enter a great circular walled courtyard, grassed in, with a central gravel path leading invitingly to the twin front doors. The house itself forms part of the curve, and two pyramid-roofed garden rooms flank the main building like guard houses. The tall, straight chimneys and the curved brick facade reminded me of a castle. Even the garden is divided into a series of rooms sheltered by tall clipped hedges which open to a paved rose garden and give vistas down green walks of a classical statue or a stone garden seat, as well as protecting the house from sea winds.

Inside there is the same feeling of haven. A promenade with armchairs in comfortable bays leads to the book-lined library, where a log fire burns cheerfully and wide settees invite relaxation. A sun lounge allows enjoyment of the rose garden even in rain and a small cosy bar was most convivial. There are two staircases, one to the main bedrooms, where Edward VII often stayed, the other to the smaller but no less comfortable rooms in the nursery wing. My room had blue walls hung with seascapes, a white bedspread and a peach-coloured easychair. A vase of daffodils, a bowl of fresh fruit, and many toiletries

were very welcome; a telephone and colour television, a sewing kit in a little basket, a bottle of Scottish spring water and a shelf of books were all thoughtfully provided. The bathroom's white wallpaper was patterned with blue cornflowers and hung with military prints. Thick white towels were plentiful and the soap was from Floris of St James's.

Luckily, Greywalls has retained its period features, such as handsome brass window catches and door fittings. Under the watchful eye of its efficient and charming manager, Henrietta Fergusson, it also preserves the feeling of a family home. Owner Giles Weaver and his wife are frequently about, since they live in a house at the end of the garden. His grandfather bought Greywalls, and his father converted it into a hotel in 1948. Famous golfing personalities can often be glimpsed in the candlelit dining room: keen players flock to Gullane, but those wishing to play at Muirfield must make their own arrangements with the secretary there well in advance of arrival. Greywalls is an architectural treasure and a golfer's delight.

Food at Greywalls is tasty and imaginative – a delicious confection of spun sugar and fresh fruits is shown above. Reception rooms are friendly and comfortable (opposite). The garden facade is pure Lutyens, both imposing and welcoming (overleaf).

GREYWALLS, Muirfield, Gullane, East Lothian EH31 2EG. **Tel.** Gullane (0620) 842144. **Telex** 72294 GREYWL G. **Owners** Mr and Mrs Giles Weaver. **Manager** Miss Henrietta Fergusson. **Open** April to Oct. inclusive. **Rooms** 19 double, 4 single, all with bathroom (with wall shower), direct-dial phone, radio and TV. **Facilities** Library, sitting room, sunroom, 2 dining rooms, small bar, 6½-acre garden, sea view. Golf at Muirfield by arrangement. Small pro/gift shop selling golfing accessories, cashmere, etc.; showcase with enamel, crystal, woollens, etc., for sale. Laundry, shoe cleaning, croquet, tennis, putting. **Lunch** Yes, but must book. **Restrictions** Men requested to wear jacket and tie in evenings. **Terms** Medium. **Credit cards** Access/Amex/Visa. **Getting there** A1 E through Musselburgh, L on A198 (signposted North Berwick) to Gullane. 18 miles, approx. ½ hr. **Helicopter landing** Yes. **Nearest airport** Edinburgh. **Nearest rail station** North Berwick. **Of local interest** Edinburgh; 13th-century Dirleton Castle ruins and garden; beaches; boat to Bass Rock and Fidra islands; castles at Tantallon and Hailes; working mill at Preston; tweed mill and shop, Haddington. **Whole day expeditions** Sir Walter Scott's home at Abbotsford and surrounding Border Country; Melrose and Dryburgh Abbeys; Berwick-on-Tweed. **Refreshments** Scott Hamilton's and Golf Inn, Gullane; Open Arms, Dirleton. **Dining out** La Potinière, Gullane.

Presidential privilege

The windows of the great drawing room of the guest apartments of Culzean Castle, high up on the cliffs, have a breath-taking sea view. At night spectacular scarlet and gold sunsets illuminate scattered bands of clouds and the jagged mountains of the Isle of Arran. At dawn, the Isle seems to float in the mist, as the sea turns from palest silver to duck-egg blue, to pink, and the first rays from the still not visible sun strike the mountain tops.

Culzean Castle was a massive defensive medieval fortress greatly lacking in comforts when it was inherited by the 10th Earl of Cassilis. With great good sense he commissioned Robert Adam in 1777 to turn it into a gracious, light-filled mansion. In the following fifteen years the great Scottish architect transformed the building with consummate taste and skill. In 1945 the earl's descendants handed the castle to the National Trust for Scotland, a private, entirely subscription-funded organization, which has lovingly restored everything to pristine perfection. After World War II, use of the apartments forming the entire top floor of the castle was passed to General Dwight D. Eisenhower for his lifetime, as a gesture of gratitude from the Scottish nation. He was several times a visitor, once as President of the United States of America. Following his death, use of the apartments reverted to the Trust, who with the help of patrons from both sides of the Atlantic, refurbished them, installing more efficient heating. Strictly by prior arrangement, these are now available for private guests.

The six spacious bedrooms are furnished with antiques and have efficient modern bathrooms with

showers. I found that even my bathroom had a splendid sea view. The vast drawing room has a well-stocked, honour-system drinks cupboard, an ice-making machine and a colour television. Commodious settees are ranged in front of the log fires in the Adam fireplaces, one at each end of the room. The dining room's long polished table glitters with period silverware and a resident steward and housekeeper oversee guests' comfort. Administrator Michael Tebbutt and his charming wife, Hazel, advise on sightseeing and arrange private visits to nearby castles, including that of the Earl and Countess of Glasgow, who joined us for dinner on the night I was staying. Golf can be played on the famous Troon and Turnberry courses nearby, with notice. Signatures in the guest book include that of Prince Charles, one of many distinguished guests to have enjoyed the exclusive experience of a visit to Culzean.

A magnificent castle and grounds (opposite, above), sumptuous four-poster beds (opposite, below) and a superb display of antique pistols (above) are part of an unforgettable ensemble.

NATIONAL GUEST APARTMENTS, Culzean Castle, Maybole, Ayrshire KA19 8LE. **Tel.** Kirkoswald (06556) 274 (guests' line 643). **Telex** No. **Owner** National Trust for Scotland. **Administrator** Michael Tebbutt. **Open** All year, except Feb. **Rooms** 6 double, 4 with own bathroom, 2 with shared bathroom (4 bathrooms have wall showers, 1 has hand shower). All bedrooms have radio. **Facilities** Self-contained top floor of castle, including drawing room, dining room. Walled flower garden, 563-acre country park with sea views and woodland walks. **Lunch** By arrangement. **Restrictions** No dogs please. **Terms** Expensive. Reduced rates for hire of entire apartment for 1 week or more. **Credit cards** Amex/Visa. **Getting there** M8 to Glasgow, A77 to Maybole. B7023, A719 to Culzean Castle. Inform attendant at entrance gate of reason for visit and no entrance fee will be charged; drive through main gateway of castle and park beside main door. 90 miles, approx. 2½ hrs. **Helicopter landing** Yes. **Nearest airport** Prestwick or Glasgow (car can collect by arrangement). **Nearest rail station** Maybole. **Of local interest** Alloway (birthplace of Robert Burns); Ayr; Scottish Maritime Museum, Irvine; Penkill Castle, Girvan; Blairquhan (see p. 89); Bargany Gardens; Casle Kennedy gardens; golf at Turnberry and Troon; Burrell Collection, Glasgow. **Whole day expeditions** Carrick Forest; Newton Stewart and Loch Trool; Glenluce; Logan Gardens; Isle of Arran and Brodick Castle. **Refreshments** Splinters, Girvan; Jock's, Kirkmichael. **Eating out** Bruce Hotel and Malin Court, Maidens; Turnberry Hotel, Turnberry (see p. 91); Fouters Bistro, Ayr; Blairquhan (see p. 89), by arrangement only; Decanters, Prestwick; The Wheatsheaf Inn, Symington.

House-party hospitality

'A most gentleman-like place, rich in all sorts of attractions – of wood, lawn, river, garden, hill, agriculture and pasture' commented Lord Cockburn when visiting Blairquhan in 1844, and so it remains.

A three-mile drive leads from the lodge through a 2500-acre park to the long grey stone castle. Medieval ruins by the riverside were demolished by architect William Burn when in 1824 Sir David Hunter Blair commissioned him to build Blairquhan on a more pleasant site, higher up the hillside, with splendid views of the Water of Girvan. Burn's classical training shows in the elegant proportions of the rooms. The tall double-storied saloon has a gallery, the small drawing room, once the billiard room, is decorated with pale green silk and an enormous drawing room overlooking the river has brocaded walls and a concert grand piano. There is a fine double staircase, a book-lined library and a magnificent dark green dining room hung with enormous family portraits and still containing the furniture made for it in 1824. Several Raeburns hang on the walls and there is a delightful family portrait by David Allan of the first baronet, Sir James Hunter, with his heiress wife, Jean Blair, and nine of their fourteen children, including David, who built Blairquhan. In the family museum of memorabilia is a tragic note pencilled by David's eldest son, James, mortally wounded at the Battle of Inkerman in 1854, bidding his father farewell. He is commemorated by an obelisk on the hillside above the house.

Housemartins were nesting under the eaves when I visited Blairquhan. The stately Red Room, in which I stayed, had a most comfortable towering four-poster bed. An antique desk was equipped with a tortoiseshell writing set and there was a red velvet chaise-longue at the foot of the bed. The twin ewers and basins on the washstand were ornamental only, since there was a private bathroom (and a dressing room as well). Only the unique carpet slightly acknowledged the passing of time. James Hunter Blair, beau ideal of all bachelor uncles, is a superb host. The enormous dining room, glittering with family silver, comes alive when he sits at the head of the table. I joined a party of friends and relatives and together we enjoyed an excellent, elegantly presented meal.

This is a private home, so you must arrange a visit well beforehand with the owner. Under his care, the house has been redecorated and impeccably maintained. Blairquhan impressively embodies family traditions lovingly preserved.

Blairquhan is a beautiful mansion in a lovely rural setting (opposite, above). Family portraits, crystal and polished wood adorn the dining room (opposite, below); the excellent food is served on antique family porcelain.

BLAIRQUHAN, Straiton, Maybole, Ayrshire KA19 7LZ. **Tel.** Straiton (0655) 7239. **Telex** No. **Owner** James Hunter Blair. **Open** All year. **Rooms** 5 double, 3 twin, all with bathrooms (4 have hand showers). 3 have single-bed dressing rooms, 1 has direct-dial phone. No TV in rooms. **Facilities** 2 drawing rooms, library, dining room, billiards room, gallery with collection of Scottish Colourists. Table tennis, croquet. 2500-acre grounds with gardens, woods, river and loch. Own stalking, shooting and fishing, by arrangement. **Lunch** By arrangement. **Restrictions** None. **Terms** Medium; no service charge but gratuities for the staff may be left in bedrooms. **Credit cards** No. **Getting there** M8/A8 towards Glasgow. After approx. 30 miles, turn L on to A725 for E. Kilbride. R on A726 (Paisley direction), then L on B764 to A77, Bypass Ayr and after 5 miles turn L on to B7045. ½ mile after Kirkmichael turn R over small bridge beside lodge and follow private drive for 3 miles. 90 miles, approx. 2 hrs. **Helicopter landing** Yes. **Nearest airport** Prestwick or Glasgow. **Nearest rail station** Maybole. **Of local interest** Culzean Castle (see p. 87); Alloway (birthplace of Robert Burns); Crossraguel Abbey; Ayr; Carrick Forest. Golf at Turnberry, Prestwick and Troon. **Whole day expeditions** Solway Firth and Loch Trool; Drunlanrig Castle; Isle of Arran. **Refreshments** Splinters, Girvan; Jock's, Kirkmichael; Black Bull, Straiton. **Dining out** Bruce Hotel, Maidens; Turnberry Hotel, Turnberry (see p. 91); Fouters Bistro, Ayr.

To the sound of the pipes

Dining at the Turnberry Hotel is a memorably delightful experience. Perched high on a hillside, the hotel overlooks golf courses, a lighthouse built on the ruins of Robert the Bruce's castle, and strange, rocky Ailsa Craig rising out of the sea. The charming, efficient, formally dressed dining room staff have magically preserved a pre-World War II stylishness of service combined with a genuine smiling welcome even for the smallest child or most unsure teenager. The food is excellent. This was the only place in Scotland where I was offered haggis as a main course on the menu, so I could not miss this delicious treat. It was preceded by a salmon mousseline with dill cream sauce, and a crab and prawn bisque. Exotic fruits with a kirsch sabayon and coffee served with home-made shortbread and fudge were also very good. During dinner, a piper in full Highland dress played while solemnly marching up and down outside the dining room window, bonnet ribbons fluttering in a stiff breeze, but undaunted.

The atmosphere of the hotel is equally likeable. The long, red-roofed and whitewashed Edwardian building was constructed in the heyday of steam railways, when keen golfers arrived by train to play the challenging courses, which have twice of necessity been transformed into airstrips and twice been totally reconstructed to championship standard. The rooms are connected by long arched corridors and most look out onto the view. Those on the upper floor have cosily sloped ceilings and dormer windows: mine felt more like a bedroom in a friend's house than in a hotel. The heavy cream-coloured bedspread matched the headboard and there was a long range of

louvered hanging cupboards. The colour scheme was a pleasing combination of green and café-au-lait shades, with touches of red in the lampshades and in the chintz curtains. The settee and easychair were comfortable and there were brass doorhandles and old prints of sailing ships. The large skylit bathroom had a marble floor, pinewood fittings and floor-to-ceiling white tiles with a tiny moss-green artichoke-shaped pattern. Big, soft fluffy white towels were heaped on a hot rail and a built-in hair drier, telephone, radio and television loudspeaker and a wicker basket brimming over with toiletries were conveniently provided. The jacuzzi bathtub and the good shower in a 'glass-fronted stall were especially welcome. This is a busy hotel, with plenty of comings and goings, but always thoughtful and attentive to the needs of its guests.

Turnberry's bright façade and warm red rooftops overlook the golf course (above). Inside, marble pillars and comfortable furniture are reminiscent of a traditional British club.

THE TURNBERRY HOTEL AND GOLF COURSES, Turnberry, Ayrshire KA26 9LT. **Tel.** Turnberry (0655) 31000. **Telex** 777779. **Operators** Orient Express Hotels. **General Manager** Christopher Rouse. **Open** Late Feb. to end Nov. **Rooms** 6 suites, 7 junior suites, 99 double, 34 single, all with bathroom (most with wall shower; 10 with jacuzzi also), direct-dial phone, radio and TV. **Facilities** Drawing room, writing room, lounge, restaurant, cocktail bar; clubhouse coffee shop, bar and restaurant; private conference and dining facilities for up to 130. 360-acre grounds, 2 championship golf courses, pro shop, putting greens, pitch and putt, beaches, tennis (2 hard courts), croquet. Stalking, shooting, fishing, horse riding by arrangement. Baby sitting, same-day laundry and dry-cleaning, beauty salon, boutique, heated indoor pool, sauna, solarium, gym, billiards, darts, table tennis, games room. **Lunch** Yes. **Restrictions** No dogs in public areas.

Terms Expensive. Reductions for children under 15; some special golfing holidays. **Credit cards** Access/Amex Diners/JCB/Visa. **Getting there** M8 to Glasgow. Follow signs to Prestwick Airport until on A77 to Turnberry. Hotel signposted on R. 95 miles, approx. $2\frac{1}{2}$ hrs. **Helicopter landing** Yes. **Nearest airport** Prestwick or Glasgow. **Nearest rail station** Girvan. **Of local interest** Robert Burns country, including birthplace at Alloway and Tam O'Shanter Museum at Ayr; Culzean Castle; Johnnie Walker Distillery, Kilmarnock; Killochan Castle and Bargany gardens; ruins of Crossraguel Abbey. **Whole day expeditions** Boat to Ailsa Craig; Isle of Arran; Carrick Forest; Glasgow. **Refreshments** Splinters, Girvan; Jock's, Kirkmichael; Black Bull, Straiton. **Dining out** Bruce Hotel, Maidens; Fouters Bistro, Ayr; Blairquhan (see p. 89), by arrangement only.

A tranquil haven

A steep valley lined with trees and yellow gorse and carpeted in spring with bluebells and primroses leads down to Knockinaam Lodge Hotel. Hidden in its 35-acre private estate, its windows look out over a pebbled beach to the sea. Built in 1869 as a holiday home for Lady Hunter Blair of Blairquhan (see page 89) and enlarged in 1901, the house was first run as a hotel by a French chef, and it is into the hands of a Frenchman, Seychelles-born Michel Frichot, that it has recently returned.

Like his English wife, Corinna, also a trained hotelier, he has rebelled against the impersonality of many big hotels. Both make a point, whenever possible, of appearing each evening to welcome their guests personally. They work hard with their young French and British staff to ensure that guests are cared for, that the food is prepared to the most exacting French standards and that everything inside and out is polished and gleaming. They also cultivate the large kitchen gardens, maintain the immaculately smooth croquet lawn and still find time to raise their young family.

Meals are simply served, but gastronomically highly memorable. Local fresh salmon was marinated in lemon juice, seasoned with coriander and chives and served with newly baked brown bread and butter. Lamb fillet, tender and garlic-flavoured, was accompanied by plenty of perfectly cooked vegetables from the garden; the mango sorbet had a raspberry coulis and was garnished with strawberries and cream. The selection of cheese was excellent, each one in a state of perfect ripeness. Coffee and handmade petits fours were served afterwards in the flower-filled sitting room, which is furnished with comfortable chintz-covered chairs. The book shelves were well-stocked, a table was heaped with current magazines and, as in most of the rooms, there was a splendid view over the sea towards Ireland. In cool weather log fires are lit in all public rooms. The Frichots have redecorated the mellow pine interiors with pretty chintzes and added a bathroom to every bedroom (one is cleverly tucked under a sloping roof), carefully preserving a massive antique bath with claw feet in which Churchill loved to wallow when he attended a secret conference with Eisenhower here during World War II.

The valley is so peaceful and secluded that deer wander out of the trees to browse in the open; in the evening a fox trotted purposefully across the lawn in full view of the diners. Bird watchers scarcely need to stir from their bedroom windows. This is the perfect place to stay if you wish to explore a surprisingly little-visited corner of Scotland or simply need to break a journey to or from Ireland. For Marcel Frichot, who has worked in and managed highly sophisticated hotels world-wide, it is a haven of tranquillity on the edge of the sea, which he shares with his family and his fortunate guests.

Opposite and overleaf: A rugged setting, beautiful food and warm, welcoming interiors – the ideal Scots experience.

KNOCKINAAM LODGE HOTEL, Portpatrick, Wigtownshire DG9 9AD. **Tel.** Portpatrick (077681) 471. **Telex No. Owners** Marcel and Corinna Frichot. **Open** Easter to New Year. **Rooms** 9 double, 1 single, all with bathroom (with hand showers), direct-dial phone, radio and TV. **Facilities** Drawing room, dining room, morning room bar. 35-acre private grounds, beach, sea views, croquet. Stalking, shooting and fishing nearby, by arrangement. **Lunch** By arrangement. **Restrictions** Dogs by arrangement only and not in public rooms; no children under 12 in dining room for dinner – but a separate high tea is provided for them instead. **Terms** Moderate. **Credit cards** Access/Amex/Diners/Visa. **Getting there** M8 to Glasgow. Follow signs to Prestwick Airport until on A77, then follow signs for Stranraer. Continue on A77 after Stranraer; hotel is on L just before Portpatrick. 130 miles, approx. 3 hrs. **Helicopter landing** Yes. **Nearest airport** Prestwick or Glasgow. **Nearest rail station** Stranraer. **Of local interest** Portpatrick; Mull of Galloway; deserted church of Kirkmadrine at Sandhead, with Romano-Christian monuments of 5th or 6th century AD; Logan gardens; Dunskey Castle; Castle Kennedy gardens. **Whole day expeditions** Culzean Castle; golf at Turnberry, Prestwick and Troon; Isle of Arran; Threave Gardens; Burns Country. **Refreshments** Crown Hotel, Portpatrick. **Dining out** Nothing nearby.

Index